GIFTS FROM THE GREEKS

Alpha to Omega

GIFTS FROM THE GREEKS

Alpha to Omega

by Sophia A. Boyer and Winifred Lubell

RAND McNALLY & COMPANY   Chicago   New York   San Francisco

Contents

The Adventurous Greeks

Athena, warrior goddess. With helmet and spear and snake-fringed breastplate (aegis), she protected her city, Athens

More than three thousand years ago Greek pirate kings sailed the Aegean Sea and raided the little cities on its shores. They began an adventure that affects us still. They were the earliest members of the remarkable Greek society, a society in which man found a sense of delight in himself and in the strange and beautiful world about him. Their fresh and lively feelings are with us today in the creations they have left us. This ancient people adventured on the sea, but were even more daring as explorers and creators in the realms of poetry, science (they discovered an atomic theory), sculpture, architecture, theater, and philosophy.

Nothing the Greeks created was ever dull. Greek temples, perched on bold headlands above the sea, are still thrilling sights, even though they are now in ruins. The sculpture that adorned those temples is exciting to see, though most of what remains is in fragments in museums. Greek dramas can compete with modern plays in our theaters. The fascinating tales, or myths, that the Greeks made up about their gods and heroes are a vital part of our literary heritage. The very words the Greeks used thousands of years ago are spoken still in everyday English. "Theater" is derived from a Greek word, as are "atom," "mouse," "geometry," "poet," "idea," "orchestra," and hundreds of others.

The Greeks were able to leave a literature because they early developed a phonetic alphabet, an important tool in building their unique society. They learned the letters of this alphabet, around the eighth century B.C., from the Phoenicians who lived in Asia Minor on the eastern coast of the Mediterranean. Phonetic writing was a revolutionary idea at that time, because the older civilizations, such as the Egyptian and Babylonian, used picture writing, in which each symbol represented a whole word. This was very awkward, since each word had to be learned separately—a task so time-consuming that only a few people ever undertook it.

With the alphabet, Greek life was speeded up in many ways. The Greeks could keep accounts and write letters which expanded trade and increased their wealth. They could preserve scientific discoveries and poems and stories. The alphabet saved for posterity the *Iliad* and *Odyssey* of Homer, two of the finest gifts of the Greeks to the world.

On the opposite page is a table of the ancient Greek alphabet. The same one is used in Greece today.

Many of these Greek letters are familiar because the Romans took over the Greek alphabet, wrote some of the letters in a new way, and made it the basis of their Latin alphabet, which we use in English.

Greek Alphabet / English Equivalents

Name of letter	Capital letter	Small letter	English equivalents		Name of letter	Capital letter	Small letter	English equivalents	
Alpha	A	α	A	a	Nu	N	ν	N	n
Beta	B	β	B	b	Xi	Ξ	ξ	X	x
Gamma	Γ	γ	G	g	Omicron	O	o	O	o
Delta	Δ	δ	D	d	Pi	Π	π	P	p
Epsilon	E	ϵ[1]	E	e	Rho	P	ρ	R	r
Zeta	Z	ζ	Z	z	Sigma	Σ	σ[3]	S	s
Eta	H	η[2]	E	e	Tau	T	τ	T	t
Theta	Θ	θ	TH	th	Upsilon	Υ	υ	U	u
Iota	I	ι	I	i	Phi	Φ	ϕ	PH	ph
Kappa	K	κ	K	k	Chi	X	χ	CH	ch
Lambda	Λ	λ	L	l	Psi	Ψ	ψ	PS	ps
Mu	M	μ	M	m	Omega	Ω	ω[4]	O	o

[1] Pronounced as *e* in "get."

[2] Pronounced as *ey* in "they."

[3] At the end of a word, ς.

[4] Pronounced as *o* in "home."

From Alpha to Omega

Footrace in the Greek Olympic Games

"The Greeks," it is said, "had a word for it." So let us take some Greek words—twenty-four, to be exact—one for each letter of the Greek alphabet, from *alpha* to *omega*. They will take us from an "athlete," who was regarded with great admiration, even awe, by the Greeks, to the "ocean," which meant to them a mysterious river flowing around the outside of the world. Among the words we shall meet on this passage from *alpha* to *omega* are those for geometry, democracy, horses, lyric poetry, nymphs, housewife, the Parthenon, actor, and philosophy. These words, and the ideas they embody, will open up to us the remarkable achievements of the ancient Greeks and give us an idea of what sort of people they were.

10

A α is for **αθλητης**, or in English letters *athletes* (pronounced *ah-thlay-táce*), an athlete.

The word for athlete is similar in Greek and in English, but the significance of the term in ancient Greek society was very different from its meaning today. To a Greek, an athlete was a splendid person, singled out by the gods for the beauty and strength of his well-trained body. The great athletic games, held in several cities of Greece, were religious festivals. The most famous, the Olympic Games, were held every four years to honor the principal Greek god, Zeus. A display of the skill and endurance of athletes was considered the finest offering one could give the gods—greater than the usual gifts of roasted meat, grain, or wine.

A winner at the Olympic Games brought the highest honor to his city, and remained for all of his life a famous personage. A great celebration was prepared for his homecoming. The hero, clad in the purple robes of an Olympic winner, rode into the city in a chariot drawn by four white horses. His attendants sang the victory song, which the greatest poets had competed for the honor of composing for him. At Athens, an Olympic victor had many privileges, including free meals in the marketplace for the rest of his life. A portion of the city wall was taken down for his triumphant entry, to symbolize the idea that a magnificent athlete offered better protection to a city than fortifications.

The Olympic Games date back to the earliest recorded history of Greece. At the beginning of the eighth century B.C.—that is, in the 790s and 780s—the celebration consisted of one day of footraces in the meadows by the river Alpheus, at Olympia. During the next two centuries many athletic events were added, and the festival expanded into a tremendous five-day event. Throughout their long history, the games brought thousands of spectators to Olympia from all of the Mediterranean world. Not only did they come from every part of Greece, but special envoys were also sent by the governments of Egypt and other countries. To make traveling to Olympia safe, a truce was declared in any war that might be going on.

The Olympic stadium is believed to have held about forty-five thousand spectators, and a hippodrome nearby, where chariot races were run, could also accommodate the entire throng. The athletes trained for ten months at home and for another month near Olympia, and the onlookers began to arrive many days before the long-awaited opening of the games. On that day, trumpets and heralds ushered the judges and special guests, including former Olympic winners, to their seats of honor. The first day was one of rituals and festivities with no athletic contests. It ended with the sacrifice of a pig to Zeus and a tremendous feast at which portions of the meat and wine were sacrificed to the gods.

The excitement of the thousands of spectators reached a high point when the trumpets sounded for the start of the second day, when the contests began. A large portion of the crowd hurried to the hippodrome to watch the finest horses in Greece take part in chariot races. Four horses pulled each chariot, and the cheering was intense as the drivers raced their light, two-wheeled craft for about ten laps around the crowded track. Meanwhile, in the stadium, the pentathlon, the Greeks' favorite contest, was taking place. It required a variety of skills, because a contestant had to enter five events. Losers in one event could not compete in the remaining ones. First came a sprint, one length of the stadium, a little more than two hundred yards. Next was the broad jump. Parts of the crowd fell silent in disappointment and others grew increasingly noisy with delight as the winners of these events went on to compete in throwing the discus and the long, thin javelin. As a final event, the remaining athletes competed in a wrestling match.

The discus and javelin throwing were accompanied by the music of flutes, for gracefulness counted toward winning. The grace of the athletes was much admired by the Greeks, who believed that develop-

This Olympic athlete wears a victor's wreath and ribbons. He carries gifts (a jug and a rabbit) given to him by admirers

13

ing the body was just as important as training the mind. The one without the other seemed to them to produce an incomplete person. The muscles of a nude body in the violent motion of sports was a favorite subject of Greek sculptors and painters. The Greeks performed all sports naked, and boasted that this habit was one of those that made them superior to other peoples. ("Gymnastics" and "gymnasium" are derived from the Greek word *gumnos*, meaning "naked.")

The adult competitors could rest on the third day, which was devoted to contests for boys. The men competed again on the fourth day in two short races and a long one of about three miles. There were also wrestling and boxing matches, and a rough sport that was a combination of the two. The last of the athletic events was a race in armor, each man wearing a helmet and leg pieces and carrying a heavy shield.

On the last day of the Olympic Games a great procession made its way up to a sacred grove on a hill. From this height the entire valley could be seen, surrounded on three sides by mountains that were often snowcapped. The events of the final day, like those of the first, were entirely religious and ceremonial. To the Greek spectators, however, watching the straining bodies of the athletes was as much a religious experience as taking part in prayers and offerings. A Greek believed that the gods were certainly watching and enjoying the games, and

Olympic events: racers, in armor, with shields and helmets;
a chariot race; a discus thrower; wrestlers; a javelin thrower.
These illustrations, and many others in this book,
were redrawn from paintings on ancient Greek pottery

that it might be the gods themselves who selected the winners. It gave them a sense of awe to have the privilege of sharing the spectacle with the immortals.

The final procession gave the thousands of marchers an opportunity to see the masterpieces of Greek sculpture and architecture which lined the route. The procession ended at the temple of Zeus, in which stood an enormous statue of the god, more than forty feet high, by the famous sculptor Phidias. The ancients called it one of the Seven Wonders of the World. At the temple, the victors were crowned with wreaths of olive leaves from the sacred grove.

The statues along the line of march (some paid for by the fines of the athletes who cheated) and buildings like small temples, called treasuries, were built and owned by the individual Greek cities. Cities in Greece were separate and independent states, and their citizens met, more often than not, only when making war on each other. But Olympia was neutral ground, being a national shrine, and there the citizens of Athens, Sparta, Syracuse, Aegina, and many other cities marched peaceably together. One of the contributions of the Olympic Games was to bring together people from isolated and widely scattered areas to engage in the great festival, thereby giving them a feeling of unity as Greeks.

B

β is for **βρωμα**, or in English letters *broma* (pronounced *bróh-mah*), food.

To raise enough food to feed their population was a desperate struggle for the Greeks, because they had the poorest farmland in all of Europe. Their country was stony, much of it covered with craggy mountains and barren, treeless hills, where the hot sun dried up everything green by early summer. Many of the farmers had to grow whatever they could on steep slopes. Vineyards for the many grapes needed for wine could be grown on such land, as could groves of the little, twisted olive trees that live many hundreds of years. The oil from olives had many uses: in place of butter in cooking, in lamps, and as an ointment, sometimes perfumed, to rub on the body after bathing.

A Greek farmer could raise a large variety of vegetables, including beets, peas, beans, onions, and lettuce; and fruits, especially figs, apples, and pomegranates. And most farmers were beekeepers, because honey was the only sweetener in ancient times. But none of these crops supplied the most important foods needed for a good diet. The barren land made poor pasture and limited the number of animals that provided meat and milk. Especially serious was the problem of producing

Harvesting olives in ancient Greece. This is redrawn from a vase painting made in 530 B.C.

17

grain, the most basic Greek food. There was an old saying that a poor man's dinner had two courses: the first of porridge and the second of porridge.

It was only in the few fertile river valleys that a Greek farmer could plant grain—usually wheat or barley. The search for soil where grain could be grown led many Greeks to move from their original homeland, which was the Greek peninsula, its islands, and the Asia Minor coast of the Aegean Sea. These colonists established new Greek cities on many shores of the Mediterranean, wherever they found fertile soil. They settled in Sicily, southern Italy, and what is now southern France, and in some parts of Spain and northern Africa. These areas remained Greek for many centuries. The lack of food had not only caused the founding of these distant cities, but it kept each of them ever afterward in contact with what the Greeks called the *metropolis*, or mother city. For hundreds of years grain was shipped from Sicily, southern France, or settlements on the Black Sea to the cities of the Greek mainland and Asia Minor where it was exchanged for olive oil and honey and wine.

The Greeks were not big eaters. They lived on a frugal diet, but it was varied enough for good health, and was probably tasty—the Greeks were famous as fine cooks. Greek cooking was admired by all the Medi-

Greek girls gathering apples. Detail from an ornate vase painting made about 460 B.C. A basket is set in front of the tree

terranean world, but especially by the Romans. Just as a rich modern family may boast of its French chef, a rich Roman family prided itself on having a Greek cook. Some of the gourmet cooking of today dates all the way back to Greek recipes, particularly any dish that is seasoned with garlic or the herb basil. Even the poor man may have had a good dish—the Greeks flavored porridge with such seasonings as herbs, lentils, or mushrooms.

Greek words for food divided a meal into two parts. *Sitos* meant bread or porridge or other food made of grain, and *opson* was whatever food was eaten with the bread. The *opson* might be cheese; or onions or other vegetables; or fish, of which the Greeks had many varieties, including shellfish; or it might be fruit. Rich people who had time for hunting enjoyed many birds—pheasant, quail, and even thrushes, which were spoken of by Greek writers as a favorite delicacy.

But only the rich could afford any kind of meat except for a special occasion. Homer's poems give a different impression, however, for they contain many descriptions of splendid feasts of roasted oxen, lambs, and pigs. It sometimes seems as if his heroes eat an ox on every page. He was, of course, describing great dinners,. and a poet is allowed to exaggerate. But there was some truth in the impression Homer gave because, in the early days about which he wrote, there was more meat

Fish was an important food to the Greeks. This painting of a boy fishing (in 520 B.C.) also shows the popular seafood

74-1126

available for a smaller population. The land was more forested and thus offered shelter to more wild animals and made the land moister so that the pastures did not dry up so early in the summer. The action over the centuries of men and goats—the one cutting down trees and the other eating all new growth—steadily denuded the hillsides.

In Homer's language of the seventh century B.C., three words were used for meals, corresponding to breakfast, lunch, and dinner. But by the fifth and fourth centuries B.C., only two were in common use, one meaning the early meal and the other the late meal. In Athens the men are described as leaving the house early in the morning either without eating or having had only a little breakfast. Lunch, too, was a slight and casual meal. At the end of the day a man came home and bathed and had his main meal with his family. By modern standards, even this evening meal was modest in Athens. The Athenians themselves commented on the few places in the Greek world where the people were what they considered heavy eaters—in neighboring Boeotia, and in Sicily, where a large meal at noon had become a custom.

When an ancient Greek did have meat it was usually pork or lamb. They could raise pigs in the barnyard and sheep and goats were able, somehow, to subsist on the rocky mountainsides. Goat's milk was made into a cheese that was widely used by most families. Larger animals

Farm scene in Greece, sixth century B.C. A farmer plows with his ox; another figure sows seeds—both tasks were hard work in the poor, rocky soil of ancient Greece

were rare and were not used for meat. Cows were almost unknown, and a horse or an ox was always a prized possession. In fact, the ownership of either animal was a measure of wealth in Athens and made a man liable to a high rate of taxation.

Oxen were a tremendous help to the farmers, particularly in pulling plows through the stubborn soil. And when the grain was harvested, oxen tramped on it for long hours to separate the kernels from the stalks. The great, plodding beasts can be seen today in the fields of Greece, for Greek farmers have continued their ancient methods of agriculture for thousands of years. While Greek city dwellers developed exciting and sophisticated ways of life—building great temples adorned with splendid sculpture, and filling huge theaters with tragedies and comedies of a kind wholly new in the world—the farmers continued their quiet, isolated life. Even wars and conquest by foreign powers often meant little to them.

Γ γ is for **γεωμετρια**, or in English letters
geometria (pronounced *geh-oh-met-reé-ah*), geometry.

Plato, a famous Greek philosopher, founded an institution at Athens called the Academy, where he taught philosophy. At its gate was a sign that read: "Let no one enter who is ignorant of geometry." The sign correctly shows the great admiration for geometry held by many Greeks besides Plato, who regarded it as the best possible training for the mind. The Greeks enjoyed bringing order to any subject, and the symmetry and logic of geometry especially pleased them.

In the early years of this century, students often spoke interchangeably of "studying geometry" or "studying Euclid." They referred to a Greek who wrote a comprehensive work on the subject about 300 B.C. Practically all geometry taught in schools today was developed by Euclid and included in his book. His principles enabled the Greeks to build fortifications and temples, and they now enable modern man to build skyscrapers, computers, and guided missiles.

Pythagoras, a Greek who made outstanding contributions to mathematics, appears in modern geometry books in connection with a theorem that bears his name. He was one of the first scholars to become convinced that the earth was round. He arrived at his mathematical studies by a curious route. He was much interested in the relations of the notes of a musical scale, and while studying music, developed a theory of numbers that he believed would explain the entire universe.

Pythagoras lived most of his life in Italy, but he grew up in Ionia, on the coast of Asia Minor, an area that produced many Greek scholars and artists. Like all the mathematicians of his day, Pythagoras would have described himself as a philosopher. These "philosophers" explored all of the fields that we now call the sciences, and they tried to conquer all knowledge at once. A geometrician who is a good example of this ambitious attempt to work in many fields is Eratosthenes. He was a poet, a literary critic, an all-around athlete, a historian, a geographer, and the director of a great library. Eratosthenes's greatest achievement in geometry was in calculating the circumference of the earth within, it is estimated, a few hundred miles of the correct figure.

Archimedes, a contemporary of Eratosthenes in the second century B.C., lived in Syracuse on the island of Sicily, and has been spoken of by the English scholar George Huxley as "so great a mathematician that it seems impertinent to praise him." Among his discoveries was the principle of the lever, which led him to say, "Give me a place to stand, and I will move the earth." Geometricians admire Archimedes for

Ancient Greek coins often commemorated the gods or famous people. This one honors Pythagoras, the mathematician who lived in the sixth century B.C. It comes from the isle of Samos, his birthplace, where his father was an engraver of coins and precious stones

the important work he did in studying the relations of spheres, cylinders, circles, and cones, and the action of gravity. But his fellow countrymen in the city of Syracuse admired him for the use to which he put his geometrical knowledge. He invented war machines that destroyed many of the ships of a Roman fleet that had come to attack Syracuse, so that the Romans were held up for two years before they succeeded in conquering the city.

These and many other scholars in ancient Greece were able to make remarkable progress in geometry and in many other subjects because the governments of the little city-states in which they lived permitted an unusual amount of freedom of speech and thought. If a person with a very adventurous mind occasionally ran afoul of a government that threatened to silence him, he could, and frequently did, move on to another city-state.

The Greeks' lasting contribution to geometry resulted not only from this freedom to study whatever and however they wished, but was encouraged also by a surprising amount of leisure that many men enjoyed. The climate and their living habits made it fairly simple to acquire the necessities of life in Greece. People lived simply in sparsely furnished houses, needed few clothes, and ate sparingly. But they obtained even more leisure from their practice of capturing slaves, Greek and foreign alike, in kidnapping expeditions and in war. Most Greek households and farms and workshops had one or two slaves, and some had a larger number, lightening the work of their masters and their mistresses.

The use of slaves was common in the ancient world. What was unique to Greece was the intellectual life the Greeks enjoyed from their resulting free time. The Greek word *schole*, from which we get "school," means both "leisure" and "learned discussion." The most sociable of people, the Greeks delighted in all kinds of talk, from exchanging gossip to serious attempts at solving the most puzzling mysteries of the universe. They recognized the great practical importance of geometry, but most of all they found it a delightful occupation. Discoveries they made, in the third and second centuries B.C., in pursuing a pastime, are the basis of textbooks in the twentieth century A.D.

Even the enlightened Greeks practiced the evil of slavery, and slaves did most of the manual work. Here they are shown in a clay pit, digging out material for the pottery whose decorations show us much of daily life in those times

 δ is for **δημοκρατια**, or in English letters *demokratia* (pronounced *day-mock-rah-teé-ah*), democracy.

In the ancient world it was normal for absolute rulers to lay down the law and for the people to obey. It was revolutionary, therefore, when the Greeks began to practice a democratic form of government. They, too, had had absolute rulers—both kings and aristocrats—and later governors who were called tyrants, but who actually were somewhat under the control of the people.

Control of the government by the people developed in most cities of Greece in the fifth century B.C., and became what was in many ways the most completely democratic democracy the world has ever seen. It is not surprising that this happened in the Greek city-states, for they were small enough to allow people to know each other and keep abreast of public affairs. To be actively involved in the city's affairs was the breath of life to the Greeks, who had a passion for politics.

The word "politics" comes from the Greek *polis*, which we translate "city-state." It is a weak and inadequate translation, but there is no equivalent of the unique Greek institution, the *polis*. The word means "city," but it also means the democratic form of government and the rights and duties of the citizens. In modern democracies the people elect representatives who act for them, but the Greeks carried on their government themselves. All citizens belonged to the legislature and thus made their own laws, and all government positions were held by private individuals serving in turn when their names were chosen by lot, as we choose jurors. This kind of direct democracy was possible because of the small size of these communities. Only three Greek city-states ever had more than 200,000 citizens.

Athens was the largest, and because it had many writers we know more details of daily life and the methods of democracy there. To an average Athenian, the business of his city was his first concern every morning. If the legislature, called the assembly, was meeting, as it did at dawn several times a month, thousands of men would stream through the city in the dim morning light to find places to sit on the ground on the slope of a hill called the Pnyx. All citizens had the right to speak and to propose anything they wanted, but usually they accepted or rejected the proposals brought in by the members of the council, which was an executive body of five hundred. If the meeting was peaceful it was over by noon. If there was a crisis about which the people were concerned, many would insist on speaking and the meeting became turbulent and went on all day.

Even when the assembly was not meeting, Athenian men set out as the sun was rising to go about their official duties. A man had little to do before leaving his house. His cloak, which had served him as a blanket during the night, was quickly draped about him, and he needed no other clothing except a pair of sandals. He might take a small amount of bread and wine by way of breakfast, but eating and bathing and leisure in general were matters for the end of the day. The morning was for work. Many men hurried out toward the circular building which housed the council. A surprising number went toward the law courts, because Athenians were famous for engaging in lawsuits, and the number of jurors needed was very large. A run-of-the-mill case had a jury of about one hundred, and an important case involved twenty-five hundred or even more, so that the decision was made by a cross section of citizens.

Both the council building and the law courts were in a huge area of the city called the *agora*. Every Greek city had an *agora;* it served a double purpose as the marketplace and as a forum where the city's political matters were hotly debated. Many citizens flocked there to learn and discuss the latest news, so that they would be prepared to play the large part expected of them by the democratic *polis*. The men gathered in all parts of the *agora*, but particularly in front of wineshops

Scenes of life in the agora—marketplace and forum of the Greek city: a boy being fitted for sandals; countrymen transporting big jars of wine or oil to the market; a fishmonger serving his customer and barbershops, and under a distinctively Greek piece of architecture, a colonnaded walk, that provided shade in which to stroll and talk. Conversation had to compete with all the noises of the market: the crowing of roosters and the squealing of pigs, the cries of farmers hawking their fruits and vegetables, and the din from carpenter shops and armor factories nearby.

The men did the household marketing, too, while in the *agora* in the morning. They handed over their food purchases to slaves to carry home to the housewives. Women never came to the *agora* and had no part in the democracy that kept the men so busy. This democracy also excluded the many foreigners who lived and worked in Athens and the slaves who made up about half of the population.

A few slaves had a curious duty on days when the assembly was meeting. They were sent out with ropes dipped in red paint to round up laggard citizens who preferred loitering in the *agora* to taking part in the legislature. Red paint on a man's cloak made him liable to a fine. Even in Athens, apparently, not every man enjoyed getting up at sunrise to act as a lawmaker. But these men were exceptions. Most Athenians were proud and eager to participate in their democracy. The Greeks had a word for a citizen who did not take part in politics. The word was *idiotes*, and has become "idiot" in English.

Drawing of a Mycenaean warrior's chariot, like those described in Homer's Iliad. This illustration is taken from a pottery fragment of the 14th or 13th century B.C.

E ε is for ʹΕλληνες, or in English letters *Hellenes* (pronounced *hél-ay-ness*), the Greeks.

The Greeks called themselves Hellenes. ("Greeks" is derived from the Roman *Graeci*.) The name comes from a mythical figure, Hellen, from whom the Greeks believed they had all descended. Historians must have envied them this simple explanation of their origin. To the historian the beginnings of Greek history were, for a long time, lost in a collection of myths and legends. There were no written accounts or definite facts on which he could rely.

Archaeology, beginning in the late 1800s, has brought to light reliable evidence from which the story of the earliest Greeks can be pieced together. With this help scholars now agree that Greek history began somewhere about 2000 B.C., when the first Hellenes began to migrate down the peninsula from the north and northeast—a process that went on for about a thousand years. About 1100 or 1000 B.C. a large new wave of Hellenes, called Dorians, came from the north and overran the whole area, driving out or destroying the larger part of the previous inhabitants. Most historians who wrote before the archaeological discoveries believed that the Dorians were the first Greeks and that any earlier inhabitants were very primitive people and were not Greek. Many books still in use give the date of the Dorian invasion for the start of Greek history.

During the time that Greek history was incorrectly dated from about 1000 B.C., people were puzzled about the Golden Age described in Homer's poems, which seemed intensely real to them but which was earlier than the Dorian invasion. To many people in many lands, the tales of the Bronze Age kings—who maintained handsome palaces in such cities as Mycenae, Tiryns, and Pylos, in southern Greece—were held to be actual Greek history. These people also believed in all the incidents of the long war at Troy of which the *Iliad* tells, when kings Agamemnon and Menelaus, the warrior Achilles, and others sailed across the sea to recover the stolen Queen Helen.

Scholars insisted that the poems were complete fiction, merely the creations of Homer's poetic imagination. But one stubborn man, Heinrich Schliemann, refused to believe that Agamemnon, Helen, Paris, and the others had never lived. He was convinced that Troy was a real city, and the Trojan War an actual event.

Schliemann began digging in Asia Minor about 1870, looking for Troy. He found a series of cities, one built on the ruins of another, one of which answered the description of the site of the Trojan War in the *Iliad*. Next Schliemann went to Mycenae, where he felt sure he could find Agamemnon's palace. Here again he was successful. His excavations uncovered a royal palace and graves full of gold and other treasure. There were still mysteries about these early people whose dwellings Schliemann had found, but no one could any longer deny that people of a considerable degree of civilization had lived in Greece before the Dorian invasion.

Archaeology since has added much to Schliemann's pioneering work, and we can picture these earliest Hellenes, who are called the Mycenaeans, in their little kingdoms in the Peloponnese, the southern portion of Greece. They lived from about 1600 to 1100 B.C., and they were the bronze-clad pirate kings who made war on each other and raided the shores of the Aegean. The Trojan War seems to have been one of the largest of these raiding expeditions. The Mycenaean kings

This bull's head is actually a ceremonial drinking cup of gold, silver, and bronze. It comes from Mycenae and was made in the 16th century B.C.

33

resembled Homer's heroes in many ways and lived in the cities and palaces he named, however much he gilded and romanticized the legends upon which he based his poems.

When the Dorians came from the north and wiped out Mycenaean life, all trace of these earliest Hellenes vanished into the earth which covers ruined cities. The Dorians themselves were a cruder people, illiterate, and unskilled in the arts of their Mycenaean predecessors. The period after their arrival, about 1100 B.C., down to about 600 B.C. is called the Dark Ages. It was a time of tumult and warfare and mingling of peoples. But during this time, and especially toward the end of it, Greek arts and literature began to develop toward the Hellenic culture that was to become famous in later centuries. In many cities craftsmen were producing fine bronze statues, lovely jewelry, and pottery covered with lively paintings. Bards roamed the land reciting epic poetry.

The Dark Ages was the only time in Greek history when the scattered cities had almost no contact with each other, because the Dorians were not seamen. The ships that sailed in and out of Greek ports were Phoenician vessels. But before the end of the Dark Ages, Greek shipping revived and the Greeks took control of commerce away from the Phoenicians. This increased seafaring was part of a great expansion of Greek prosperity and population, and it was the period in which the

Hellenes spread out over the shores of the western Mediterranean, as Plato put it, "like frogs round a pond."

The Hellenes were fortunate in having many centuries of peace in which to grow and develop. The older Egyptian and Mesopotamian civilizations of the Mediterranean world, though far more powerful than the little Greek tribes, were not great seafarers and posed no threat to people across the Aegean waters. And the Phoenicians were sailors and traders, not conquerors. But in time an enormous, aggressive power, the Persian Empire, began steadily swallowing up its neighbors, including the Greek cities of Ionia. It seemed that only a miracle could save Greece from destruction by this colossal force.

The Athenians had attempted to help the Ionian cities in Asia Minor, and in 490 B.C. the Persians sent a large expedition to punish them. The Athenians, almost single-handedly, administered a decisive defeat to the Persians at Marathon, where an Athenian army of about 10,000, with 1,000 allies, is said to have killed 6,400 Persians, losing only 192 men themselves. Ten years later, the Persian king Xerxes sent an even larger expedition of 1,000 ships and at least 100,000 men (some say many more) to conquer the Greeks.

The expert seamanship of the Athenians made it possible for them to trap the Persian fleet at Salamis and sink most of its ships. This shat-

Archer, from the decoration on an Athenian plate of the sixth century B.C. The costume resembles those of the Persian warriors whom the Athenians defeated at Marathon

tered the strength of Xerxes's tremendous expedition and ended the threat to the independence of Greece, but not before the city of Athens was invaded and burned in 480 B.C. The Spartans joined with the Athenians in this struggle, and their heroism at Thermopylae has gone down in legend. Leonidas, the Spartan king, and three hundred soldiers held off a huge Persian force at a narrow pass in the mountains for several days and nights—to give the Greek armies much-needed time—until every Spartan soldier was dead. Tourists today visit a monument marking this spot at Thermopylae.

The end of the Persian Wars in 479 B.C. left some of the cities of Greece united under the leadership of Athens, which had become outstanding in wealth and culture. It was the first time that one Greek city was dominant over the others. But the restless Hellenic peoples could not long maintain even this moderate amount of unity, and in 431 B.C. war broke out between the chief rivals, Athens and Sparta, and continued at intervals until 404 B.C., when Athens was defeated by the well-trained armies of Sparta.

The city of Thebes challenged the supremacy of Sparta for a time, but the intercity warfare was soon interrupted by a stronger power from the north. Philip, king of Macedon, and his son, Alexander the Great, had been admirers of the Athenian philosophers, and Alexander

The Ancient Greek World

BLACK SEA

Danube R.

THRACE

MACEDONIA

Byzentium. Bosporus

Rome

TYRRHENIAN
SEA

Taranto

Mt. Olympus

ASIA MINOR

THESSALY

AEGEAN

Troy

IONIAN

Strait of

SEA

Thermopylae

LESBOS

Pergamum

PHRYGIA

SICILY

Messina

SEA

ITHACA

Delphi.

SEA

LYDIA

Carthage

Mycenae.

Thebes

Marathon

Sardes

Syracuse

Olympia

Corinth

Athens

Samos

IONIA

Argos Tiryns

Aegina DELOS

Pylos.

Sparta

CYCLADES

Miletus

MELOS

RHODES

TIGRIS R.

PERSIA

Euphrates R.

Knossos

CYPRUS

Salamis

SYRIA

CRETE

Tyre.

PHOENICIA

Dead
Sea

ARABIA

M E D I T E R R A N E A N   S E A

LIBYA

Alexandria

Nile

E G Y P T

had studied with them. But Philip ended the great period of Athenian life, in which these philosophers had flourished, when he conquered all of Greece in 338 B.C.

Philip's conquest incorporated the Greek cities, which had been proudly independent for so long, into a huge empire, one that Alexander would extend to the east to include parts of India. But after Alexander's death this empire fell apart, while even greater empire-builders were developing in Italy to the west. The Romans defeated the Macedonians about 200 B.C. and took over Greece. This began two thousand years of foreign rule for the Hellenes. For many centuries they were part of the Byzantine Empire, which formed the eastern half of the Roman Empire. The Turks conquered the whole Balkan Peninsula, including Greece, in A.D. 1453, and at that time broke up the Byzantine Empire. The Greeks won their independence from the Turks in 1829. The English poet Byron was among volunteers from various countries who came to help fight for the independence of Greece, because of their devotion to the ancient culture of that land.

The Greeks themselves, as soon as they were again independent, named their country the Kingdom of Hellas, because the name represented to them their former greatness, the memory of which they had cherished during all the centuries of foreign domination.

Z

ζ is for **Ζευς**, or in English letters *Zeus* (pronounced *zeh-oóse*), Zeus.

Zeus was the leader of twelve Greek gods and goddesses, who were called the Olympians. Olympus, a high mountain in the north of Greece, was supposed to be their home. There were a great number of other Greek divinities, but none so important and well known as the Olympians. Most of the Greek gods represented some aspect of nature, including Zeus, who was the god of the upper air, with the eagle as his symbol. Like the heavens, he was often serene and benign, but could be a bringer of storms. When he was angry with men, he hurled thunderbolts down upon them.

The gods and goddesses had a splendid time on Olympus, enjoying much music and dancing and laughter, and feasting on a special food called ambrosia and imbibing a drink called nectar. This ideal life was occasionally disturbed by violent and childish quarrels. The cause of

Birth of Athena. The goddess Athena, fully armed, emerges from the aching head of Zeus, seated on his throne. The goddesses of childbirth hold his head. The scene is from a Greek dish painted about 570 B.C.

Aphrodite, goddess of love and beauty, as shown in a painting on a drinking cup of the sixth century B.C. The swastika was a traditional Greek decoration. The dove was sacred in Aphrodite's worship

many of these quarrels was Zeus's tendency to fall in love with goddesses, nymphs, and even mortals, which made his wife, Hera, very angry.

Besides Zeus and Hera and seven sons and daughters, the twelve Olympians included two brothers and one sister of Zeus. The loveliest Olympian was Zeus's daughter Aphrodite, the goddess of beauty, love, and marriage. She is often pictured at the moment of her birth, when she rose from the foam of the sea. Hephaestus, the god of fire, on the other hand, was the least attractive. He was lame, and was apt to be dirty from his work at the forge where he made armor and did other kinds of metalwork. But Hephaestus was a comic character who provided much fun and laughter for the gods and goddesses.

Athena, a favorite daughter of Zeus, was in charge of the skills of handicrafts, and being also the goddess of war she is usually portrayed with a helmet and spear. Zeus's daughter Artemis and son Apollo were twins, and both were great hunters. Artemis, who never married, was a wild and solitary creature who ranged the hills. Greek girls, just before marriage, offered their toys, dolls, and other childish belongings to her. Apollo had many roles—he was the god of light, opposed to all creatures of darkness; the god of healing; the god of prophecy; and the god of inspiration, especially of music.

40

All primitive peoples made up myths in attempting to explain the nature of the alarming and puzzling world. The Greeks inherited some of their myths from civilizations to the east, and this heritage included demons and horrible monsters. But the Greeks later discarded most of these monsters, and their religion never had any devil. Hades, the underground world of the dead, was not a real hell, but simply the abode of departed spirits. The Hellenic gods and goddesses were far less frightening than those of most early peoples. They differed little from ordinary men and women except that they were more powerful and were immortal.

Although there was then no Greek church and no religious creed, the Greeks were a very devout people who felt that their gods were always near and guiding their lives, so that it was never safe to risk offending them by failing to carry out the proper rituals. Each family performed its worship privately, often at the family altar that was in every house. At meals, a prayer and a libation of wine were offered, and often a portion of the food, first to Hestia, because she was the goddess of the home, and then to any other god who was appropriate. A libation was made to the god of sleep at bedtime.

More elaborate sacrifices of chickens, sheep, pigs, and goats—in large numbers if a man was rich enough—were made at the important

Artemis, virgin goddess of the hunt, twin sister of Apollo. She is shown with quiver, bow, arrow, and a deer on this jug of 660 B.C. from Melos

41

milestones of life: birth, marriage, death, and many others. Before planting his crops, a farmer always sacrificed to Demeter, a sister of Zeus and the goddess of the earth and of growing things. The start of a sea voyage would be unthinkable to a Hellene without his first having made offerings and prayers to Poseidon, the powerful god of the sea.

Many of the lesser gods, goddesses, and other spirits lived in the countryside. Nymphs haunted trees and streams; satyrs—creatures with hooves like those of goats—dwelt in woods and pastures. Headed by their leader, Pan, satyrs could bring good or bad luck to a potter's workshop or a smith's forge or to the flocks and herds. Since prayers were offered at all the places inhabited by these spirits, altars were to be found throughout the Greek countryside—in fields, beside streams, or on the seashore where Nereids (sea nymphs) played in the waves, as well as in the *agora* of every city.

Greeks worshiped together only at public meetings and festivals at the national shrines. Delphi, perhaps the most important of these shrines, was sacred to Apollo and contained an oracle through which the god was thought to answer the questions of mortals and give them guidance. All kinds of Greeks, but especially statesmen, consulted the oracle at Delphi. It had such prestige that even Persian kings journeyed to it from across the Aegean Sea. The words of the oracle were supposed to be those of Apollo, and were spoken through a priestess, called the Pythia. She went into a sort of fit or frenzy and gave forth incoherent, ambiguous statements that were then interpreted by a priest and put into verse by a poet.

Greek priests maintained the great shrines—Delphi, Olympia, and others—and they also saw that all rituals were properly carried out. But they were government officials similar to those responsible for overseeing commerce or education. It was not the duty of a priest to censure the morals of the people or to tell them what to believe. This religious toleration left the Greeks, especially the philosophers, remarkably free to adventure in the world of science and to seek scientific explanations of the world to replace the supernatural explanations embodied in their marvelous myths.

Ritual sacrifice of a pig shown on a vase painting from the sixth century B.C.

H η is for Ἡρακλης, or in English letters *Herakles* (pronounced *hay-rah-kláce*), Heracles.

He is better known by his Roman name of Hercules. He was so much the most famous of Greek heroes that there was an old Greek saying, "There is nothing without Heracles." His name was turned into the adjective "herculean," expressing the hero's extraordinary strength. It is possible that Heracles was an actual person, perhaps born in Thebes, as some tales say. But with the telling and retelling, century after century, of the many stories about him, his feats grew more and more miraculous and beyond the powers of any human.

The myths ascribe Heracles's many troubles to the enmity of Zeus's wife, Hera, who was jealous because Heracles was the son of Zeus and a mortal, Alcmene. Alcmene had another son, Iphicles, by her mortal husband, Amphitryon, a Theban chieftain. Though the boys were the same age, like twins, the superiority that a divine father gave to Heracles showed while he was still an infant. As the two babies lay in their bed one evening, Hera sent two deadly snakes to kill Heracles. Alcmene and Amphitryon heard screams, and rushing in found Iphicles terrified, but Heracles laughing and holding the snakes he had killed.

The enormous strength that permitted Heracles to achieve marvels also brought him disasters. When still a boy he killed his music teacher in a fit of temper or madness—some myths say a madness caused by Hera. Another such fit brought the greatest tragedy of Heracles's life, when he killed his beloved wife and children. In remorse he went to Eurystheus, king of Argos, to ask how he could expiate his terrible crime. Eurystheus gave him twelve labors to purify himself of guilt. Any one of these labors would have been impossible for a hero with less than Heracles's incredible strength and fortitude.

The first of his tasks was to bring to Eurystheus the body of the great lion of Nemea, which was impervious to any weapon. Neither Heracles's arrows nor the great club he always carried could wound it. In the end, Heracles strangled it with his bare hands and ever afterward wore its skin.

A mad bull was terrorizing the island of Crete, and Heracles was instructed to kill it, also. He did so, and carried the body across the sea on his back. Next came a beast called a hydra, with nine heads. Whenever one of its heads was cut off, two more grew in its place. But eventually Heracles overcame this monster, too.

Heracles's labors took him to many places, including Hades, where he was sent to capture Cerberus, a three-headed dog that guarded its

One of the famous feats of Heracles: overcoming the nine-headed hydra

45

gates. Another task was to bring back golden apples from the islands of the Hesperides in the Atlantic Ocean, an alarming place to the Hellenes. On his way he came to the western end of the Mediterranean, where Africa and Europe nearly meet at Gibraltar. Heracles is supposed to have pushed the two continents apart at that point, and the heights on either side are still called the Pillars of Heracles. But some of the myths say Heracles did not continue to the Hesperides, because even his courage failed at the thought of the unknown ocean. Atlas, a giant, stood on the African shore, holding the world on his shoulders, and Heracles persuaded Atlas to go to the Hesperides for the apples, while he took up Atlas's burden of holding up the world.

Anthropologists believe that Heracles's marvelous feats symbolize the attempts of the Greeks to free themselves from early forms of religion dominated by terrifying monsters. In all of the tales Heracles uses his power to protect men from demons and monstrous beasts. This greatest of Greek heroes suffered so many trials and ordeals that it is a relief to find that at the end of his life he was allowed to go up to Olympus, as if he were a god. There he married Hebe, a lovely daughter of Zeus and Hera.

Greek public buildings were almost always decorated with sculpture which depicted the gods, the heroes, and great events. Much of this art appeared on the triangular pediments above the columns of temples, as did the marble sculpture shown here. It stood originally, with other figures, on the temple of Aphaia at Aegina. It shows the hero Heracles as an archer. He wears a helmet made from the skin of the Nemean lion, which he strangled with his bare hands. The figure was carved about 490 B.C. and probably held a bow in its hands. Though broken in places it was restored by the sculptor Thorwaldson

Θ *θ* is for **θαλασσα**, or in English letters *thalassa* (pronounced *thah-láh-sah*), the sea.

Greece was as inviting and well adapted for seafaring as it was rugged and difficult for land travel. Almost everywhere along the Greek coast were harbors, large and small, where boats could run in and be anchored or pulled up on a beach, safe from gales and storms. Even as boys, many Greeks learned to manage small boats and to cope with changeable winds and currents and the reefs and other dangers of local waters. This life tended to make self-reliant and adventurous men, men not afraid to pick up and sail away in search of new homes in a better land. In their self-reliance the Greeks resembled the American frontiersmen, who continually pushed westward across this broad continent.

The earliest ships that we know about in which the Greeks took to the sea were what Homer called "hollow ships." They were much like large, open dories with only partial decks. Oarsmen rowed if the

Early depiction of a Mycenaean ship

wind failed and the sails could not be used. Life was uncomfortable aboard, and the sailors beached the boats at night, whenever possible, and slept ashore.

Discomfort was not the most serious problem of sailing before the days of compasses, charts, and maps. In the Aegean Sea it was often possible to move from island to island, keeping land always in sight. But the Greeks took other voyages that involved many days, and even weeks, of crossing open water. Then the only guides were the sun and the stars, which were useless in cloudy, rainy, or foggy weather. Greek seamen knew well the stars and constellations and how to steer by them, as Odysseus is described as doing in the *Odyssey*:

> Now the great seaman, leaning on his oar,
> steered all the night unsleeping, and his eyes
> picked out the Pleiades, the laggard Ploughman,
> and the Great Bear, that some have called the Wain,
> pivoting in the sky before Orion;
> of all the night's pure figures, she alone
> would never bathe or dip in the Ocean stream.

A later and larger Greek ship with many rowers. The original of this drawing was made in the tenth century B.C. The figures may be Helen of Troy and Paris. Another type of Greek ship is shown on page 2. These two galleys, under sail, appeared on a cup made by the potter-painter Nicosthenes in 520 B.C. His name appears on the upper right

49

Seafaring was a necessity for the Hellenes, so many of whom lived on islands or on distant shores, from the Black Sea to Spain. Very few of the Greek cities were self-sustaining, but depended on ships to bring them food and goods of all kinds. The older cities, such as Athens and Corinth, exchanged their fine metal wares and pottery and olive oil with newer cities having grain to sell. This trade in staple foods and manufactured goods was carried on in large merchant vessels that sailed the year around.

In addition, many a Greek went to sea in the safe summer season in a small boat that he had built himself. A farmer, for instance, often found the sea the best route by which to take his produce to market. If he went farther than the nearest city—to an island or distant shore—he often filled his empty ship for the return trip with any loot he could lay his hands on—sheep or oxen, or even boys and girls kidnapped to sell as slaves. Fishermen usually went considerable distances. Their favorite fishing grounds were the Black Sea and the rivers running into it. The Aegean had so little vegetation on its bottom that it could not support many fish.

An ancient Greek thought of the dangers and hardships of the sea not as battles with wind and wave, but with the wrath of Poseidon, god of the sea, or with Boreas, the north wind. Homer describes how

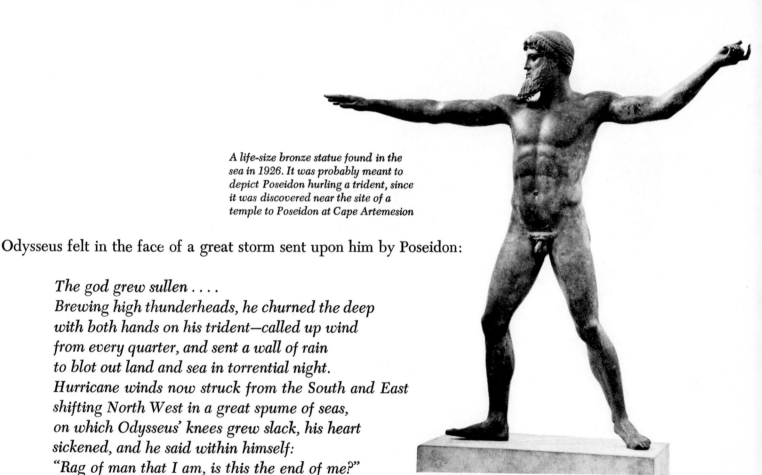

A life-size bronze statue found in the sea in 1926. It was probably meant to depict Poseidon hurling a trident, since it was discovered near the site of a temple to Poseidon at Cape Artemesion

Odysseus felt in the face of a great storm sent upon him by Poseidon:

The god grew sullen . . . .
Brewing high thunderheads, he churned the deep
with both hands on his trident—called up wind
from every quarter, and sent a wall of rain
to blot out land and sea in torrential night.
Hurricane winds now struck from the South and East
shifting North West in a great spume of seas,
on which Odysseus' knees grew slack, his heart
sickened, and he said within himself:
"Rag of man that I am, is this the end of me?"

51

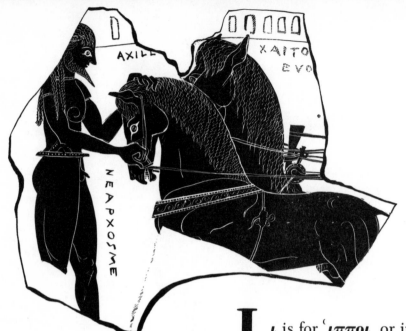

Achilles with his horses. This drawing is taken from the fragment of a drinking cup signed by Nearchos, a famous Greek potter-painter of the sixth century B.C.

I ι is for ῾ἱπποι, or in English letters *hippoi* (pronounced *híp-poy*), horses.

Homer refers to the Hellenes as "tamers of horses" and "breeders of horses," and fills his poems with descriptions of these spirited animals. In this he was typical of Greek writers who, like Greek artists and sculptors, seemed to delight in portraying horses. In real life in Greece, a horse was a rare animal, but he was far from rare in ancient Greek art or literature.

52

When Homer wrote of horses—and, indeed, of humans—he made little distinction between mortals and immortals. Achilles, the hero of the *Iliad,* had a human father and a sea nymph for a mother, and he owned both mortal and immortal horses. He had an extraordinary pair of immortal horses, Xanthos and Balios, that were born of the west wind. They had been given to Achilles's father by Poseidon, and they were driven and cared for by Patroclus, Achilles's charioteer and closest friend. He "many times anointed their manes with soft olive oil, after he had washed them in shining water." After the death of Patroclus the grief of these horses is described: "Their manes are swept along the ground as they stand with hearts full of sorrow, and hot tears drop from under their eyelids."

On one occasion Hera gave Xanthos a voice. After a scolding from Achilles, the horse responded by predicting Achilles's early death. Achilles answered that he well knew he was going to die young, but that it was not for Xanthos, a horse, to tell him so. Achilles sometimes harnessed Xanthos and Balios with a horse called "unfaulted Pedasos," who had a more lowly ancestry. But at such times, the poem says, "he, a mortal horse, kept pace with the immortal pair."

Centaurs were creatures in Greek mythology with the bodies and legs of horses and the heads and torsos of men. They were violent and disagreeable beings. Pegasus, another mythical creature, was a marvelous flying horse, as admirable and agreeable as the centaurs were horrid. No one could catch or ride Pegasus, until Athena gave a young man named Bellerophon a golden bridle with which to tame him. Mounted on Pegasus, Bellerophon was able to perform tremendous feats that almost rivaled those of Heracles. But he became so filled with pride—the sort of arrogant pride leading to a downfall which the Greeks called *hubris*—that he was undone. He had decided to ride Pegasus up onto Olympus, but the horse, knowing that this would be wrong for a mortal, threw his rider. Bellerophon thereafter lived out a miserable life on earth, while Pegasus was accepted onto Olympus.

Here Pegasus became a favorite of the gods. Zeus always asked Pegasus to bring him thunderbolts when he planned to throw them. There were stables on Olympus where Pegasus lived with the horses of the gods. Many gods and goddesses occasionally used horsedrawn chariots, but for Helios, the sun god, a chariot was a daily necessity. His was pulled by four strong horses up the sky from the east each morning and down to the west in the afternoon. There Helios stabled his horses and took a golden raft to return to the east. The west, therefore, was often called by the Greeks "the stabling place of the sun."

Left: *Helios, the sun god, with his four horses.*
Lower left: *A centaur, as depicted in a detail from a famous Greek wine jar known as "The François Vase."*
Below: *This drawing, taken from an engraved bronze plaque of the seventh century B.C., shows Bellerophon, mounted on Pegasus, attacking the monster Chimaera*

A small but very rare and famous statue of the Cretan snake goddess, made of gold and ivory. In her hands are two golden snakes. It is very old—about 1600 B.C.

K κ is for **Κρητη**, or in English letters *Krete* (pronounced *kráy-tay*), Crete.

When the Mycenaeans came to live on the Greek peninsula they found exciting neighbors living on the island of Crete to the south of them. Crete was probably inhabited as early as 3500 B.C. by a people with an amazingly sophisticated way of life. Their civilization reached its height about 1500 B.C. and included luxuries not seen again in Europe for thousands of years.

These early Cretans are called Minoans, because their kings all seem to have been named Minos. They paved and drained the roads on the island and built enormous sprawling palaces. These palaces had large, enclosed areas for sports and for sunbathing and relaxing, and were equipped with hot and cold baths. The queen's chamber even had a flush toilet. Frescoes covered the walls of the palaces, and the bits that remain show a gay life for both men and women. Archaeologists have found chess sets, many types of cosmetic jars, ladies' mirrors, and splendid jewelry. The ladies in the murals had elaborately arranged hair and wore dresses with tight bodices and long, flounced skirts. They had such an elegant air that a French archaeologist exclaimed, when he first saw the murals, "Why, these are Parisian ladies!"

Handsome bulls are so frequent in Minoan sculpture and painting as to indicate the existence of a sort of cult, part of which was a dangerous sport for the Minoan youths. Both girls and boys seized the horns of the lowered head of an onrushing bull and, as he raised his head, leaped on his back and then into the arms of a waiting partner.

The Mycenaeans on the mainland, a simpler people, were much influenced by the sophisticated Minoans, as is shown by a strong similarity in their pottery, paintings, jewelry, and other arts. The sea between them would have been no great obstacle, as both peoples were fine seamen. When the Dorians overran the Greek peninsula about 1100 B.C., the Minoan cities of Crete were destroyed at the same time as those of the Mycenaeans, and only legends remained of the Cretans.

The best-known legend is that of King Minos, who kept a terrible beast—half man and half bull—called the Minotaur in a labyrinth in his palace. Every year he fed it seven Athenian youths and seven Athenian maidens. Theseus, a hero of Athens, concealed himself among these young people and succeeded in killing the dreaded Minotaur. He was able to escape alive from the labyrinth because Ariadne, Minos's daughter, gave him a ball of string to unwind as he went into the maze, so that he could find his way out again.

Three thousand years after its sudden end, the remains of the Minoan civilization began to be unearthed. In 1900, at Knossos, the principal city of Minoan Crete, an Englishman named Sir Arthur Evans started to excavate. He had come to Crete to study ancient languages, but his archaeological discoveries were so exciting that he remained in Crete for the rest of his life (he died in 1941 at the age of ninety), digging up and restoring the enormous palace of Knossos.

In spite of the new facts revealed by Schliemann about the Mycenaeans and by Evans about the Minoans, many puzzling questions remained about the history of the two peoples. Were they two separate peoples? Sir Arthur Evans thought not. He was so absorbed in the Cretans that he considered the life on the Greek mainland simply as an extension of Cretan life. He persuaded many, but not all, scholars to this point of view. It was not until 1952 that a brilliant feat of deciphering a previously unreadable language provided a key that unlocked many of the puzzles about this early period.

Evans had found two types of clay tablets with writing on them that no one could read, which he called Linear A and Linear B. Close study had shown that, though written in the same symbols—which represented syllables, not letters—their differences were great enough to indicate two separate languages. Linear A was found all over the island of Crete but nowhere else. Linear B was found only at Knossos on Crete, but turned up in many Mycenaean cities on the Greek peninsula. A young English architect, Michael Ventris, had been fascinated by these tablets since the age of thirteen, when he had heard Evans lecture about them. By the time he was eighteen, Ventris had published a learned paper on the subject. In 1952, only a few years before his death in an auto accident at the age of thirty-four, he succeeded in deciphering Linear B. Ventris was astonished to find that what he had been working on was an early form of Greek. The tablets were tax lists and shipping accounts, and so told only indirectly about the people who wrote them.

Michael Ventris's discovery proved that people who spoke and wrote Greek were the inhabitants of the Mycenaean cities where Linear B tables were found. Linear A has not yet been deciphered, but it was obviously the language of the Minoans, and so Ventris's discovery shows that they were a separate, non-Greek people. The fact that the Greek Linear B writing appears at Knossos, but only at a late date, has persuaded historians that the Mycenaeans, the followers and imitators of the Minoans, in the end conquered their teachers. Once the Mycenaeans were established at Knossos and in control of the great Minoan trade routes, they had a need for writing to carry on their ex-

Figure in a fresco painting depicting a sacrifice. It was found in Minoan Crete on a sarcophagus of the 15th century B.C.

Acrobat on a bull. Drawn from a small bronze figure found in Minoan Crete

tensive commerce. They used the symbols of Linear A to write down their own Greek language.

The achievements of Schliemann, Evans, and Ventris are only dramatic high spots in the story of the long years of careful archaeological work by many scholars that has unearthed the lost civilizations of Minoan Crete and Mycenaean Greece. A large Minoan city which had been buried under the ash of a volcanic eruption was discovered in the summer of 1967 on the island of Thera, just north of Crete. Only a beginning has been made in digging out this city. When more of it is excavated, and if other such cities are found, we can hope to learn more about the Cretans, who were playing chess, vaulting over bulls, and living in splendid palaces while the peoples of the rest of Europe dwelt in caves.

A music lesson in 480 B.C.

 λ is for **λυρα**, or in English letters *lura* (pronounced *loó-rah*), a lyre.

The lyre was an extremely ancient musical instrument used by the Greeks, and by earlier eastern peoples. An ancestor of the harp, it had seven strings that were usually stretched on a tortoise shell. A lyre is frequently shown in the hands of Apollo, the god of music. He played it to entertain the gods when they feasted on Olympus. Men, and

61

even animals, were also charmed by Apollo's lyre. The playwright Euripides describes leopards and lions as coming from the forest and following Apollo harmlessly while he played, and "a spotted doe danced on light hoofs."

When Apollo played his lyre for the immortals, he was often accompanying the singing of a group of nine goddesses called the Muses. They were not inhabitants of Olympus, but lived on the tops of various other mountains. At night they often wrapped themselves in clouds and came down to where men could hear their lovely voices. Each Muse had a particular art—such as epic poetry, religious music, or tragedy—under her special charge, but all were goddesses of inspiration.

"Any art presided over by the Muses," is part of the definition in Greek dictionaries of the word *mousike*. It makes us think of "music," which we derive from it, but the Greek word includes much more besides music. It includes everything sung to a lyre, which means almost all of Greek literature. Poetry and drama were, in early times, always accompanied by music. Epic poetry was sung or chanted to the chords of a lyre to entertain kings and their guests in their palaces. When monarchy gave way to democracy, the bards recited the epics before huge audiences at the festivals in the cities.

A different type of poem was sung to the music of the lyre by large choruses of men or boys. These poems, called odes, were a central part of the religious rituals. The poet, it was believed, composed them under the inspiration of a god, and his ode explained the ritual and the significance of the occasion to the people. The Pythian Games, held at Delphi, were almost as famous in ancient times as the Olympics. But since Delphi was the shrine of Apollo, the god of music, the contests involved choral odes as well as athletic events.

Learning to play the lyre was a very important part of an Athenian boy's education. He was learning in this way the tales of his heroic Hellenic ancestors in the epic poems, and the odes taught him much about religious observances. Not only was music called by the Greeks the most basic part of education, but they considered music to be the greatest of all arts, ranking it above architecture, sculpture, painting, or literature. The world has suffered a great loss, then, because ancient Greek music has disappeared completely. We have only the words remaining of what was once a performance in which the music, words, and dancing were inseparable.

Pindar, the most famous of the writers of choral odes, addresses the lyre in a poem written for Hieron, who had won the music contest at the Pythian Games. Pindar called the lyre powerful enough to

Greek youth with a lyre

63

Apollo with his great lyre, probably the type called a cithara. This detail is taken from the painting on a wine jug

overcome Zeus, for he means the god himself when he speaks of the eagle and the thunderbolt, Zeus's symbols:

Oh, golden lyre, possessed equally by Apollo
and the violet-haired Muses,
the dancers' step listens for you . . .
and singers, too, obey the signal
of your throbbing strings. . . .
You quench the everlasting fire of the warlike
thunderbolt. On the scepter of Zeus the eagle
sleeps, his strong wings drooping on either side—
the king of birds—you have poured a cloud on his
black face and beaked head, and gladly his
eyelids he has closed.
His lithe back ripples as he sleeps,
held by the onrush of your song.

Mμ is for **μελη**, or in English letters
mele (pronounced *mél-ay*), lyric poetry.

Most Greek poetry might be called "public" poetry because it told of
the gods and heroes and so expressed the patriotic and religious feelings of all the people. The poet's own feelings had no place in that kind
of poetry. But in lyric poetry the poet was not writing on behalf of all
of his fellow citizens and could express his private emotions.

Sappho, Greece's greatest woman poet, was an outstanding writer
of lyric poetry. Her poems have a modern ring because the poignant
feelings of which she wrote are universal feelings, as keenly felt by
people today as by the Hellenes so long ago. Typical of her work is this
brief verse about loneliness:

> *The moon is down*
> *and the Pleiades.*
> *It is midnight.*
> *Time is passing,*
> *and I lie alone.*

One of the Muses. To ancient Greeks, the
Muses were the inspiration for poetry
and music. Detail taken from an Attic cup

Lyric poems were a frequent verse form in Greece in the Dark

Ages, from about 750 to 600 B.C. Alcman was a Spartan poet who wrote in this period, which was before the Spartan state banned all poetry as weakening to the militaristic spirit required of its citizens. Alcman was not a Spartan citizen, but a slave brought there from his native Asia Minor. Like many slaves he was more literate than his masters, and he wrote many odes for Spartan festivals. The informal subject of this poem by Alcman is certainly not in the stern Spartan tradition:

Often upon the mountain peaks
where noisy feasts delight the gods,
then did you take a great gold pan,
the sort of pan that shepherds use,
and milked a lioness with your hands
to make a great unbroken shining cheese.

Only a very small fraction of Greek lyric poetry has survived the centuries. Manuscripts were of papyrus, and many are now only tantalizing fragments. From time to time lyric poems have turned up in Egypt, where the dry climate has kept papyrus from disintegrating and where many Greek writings were collected in a great library at Alexandria. The most surprising place where Greek poems have been found

Shepherd on a goat, playing his flute

is inside of crocodiles! The Egyptians made mummies of sacred crocodiles to put into tombs, and used papyrus, cut into long, thin strips, as stuffing, oblivious to any writing that might have been on the papyrus. Scholars were confronted with the formidable task of piecing together the strips so as to reconstruct the poems written on them.

Many of Sappho's poems are in bits and pieces—sometimes a whole short verse, but often only a line, or even a word or two. Not much is known about Sappho's life, except that she lived on the island of Lesbos off the coast of Asia Minor in the sixth century B.C., and she had a school for girls. She often wrote haunting poems about simple events of everyday life, like this one:

My mother always said
that in her youth she was
exceedingly in fashion
wearing a purple ribbon
looped in her hair. But
the girl whose hair is yellower
than torchlight need wear no
colorful ribbons from Sardis,
but a garland of fresh flowers.

Greek girl in a fine dress, with a garland in her hair. From a painted jar, 520 B.C.

67

And here is another Sappho poem:

> *Evening, you bring all things which*
> *the bright dawn scattered.*
> *You bring the sheep, you bring the goats,*
> *you bring the child to its mother.*

Many Greek poems are epitaphs. This is by an unknown writer, about the death of a lonely farmer:

> *Naiads and cold ox-pastures*
> *tell to the bees when they come*
> *on their springtime way*
> *how old Leucippus died on a cold*
>   *winter's night,*
> *lying in ambush for scampering hares.*
> *No more the beehives can he tend with love.*
> *The wooded dells long much for him,*
> *and the high peak that was his neighbor.*

Greek potter-painters, like the poets, delighted in portraying the details of country life. The animals shown here are typical of their work. The round drawing from a cup shows birds in a tree, a nest, and even a grasshopper

N ν is for $\nu\nu\mu\phi\alpha\iota$, or in English letters *numphai* (pronounced *noóm-phigh*), nymphs.

The nymphs were spirits between true goddesses and human beings, who inhabited many places in the countryside. Dryads lived in trees; Naiads were the nymphs of springs and streams; Oreads were mountain nymphs; Pereia, rock nymphs; and Nereids, sea nymphs—to mention only a few. All were beautiful maidens, fond of singing and dancing.

Most of the myths about nymphs tell of their adventures when one of the powerful Olympic gods, such as Zeus, Poseidon, or Apollo, fell in love with them. Some myths grow from the desire of Greeks in various areas of the country to trace their descent from a god, through an ancestor who was a child of Zeus or Poseidon and a nymph. In Arcadia there was such a story of a remarkably beautiful nymph named Callisto, who hunted with Artemis and with whom Zeus was in love. She and Zeus had a son, Arcas, from whom all the Arcadians were thought to descend. Hera, in a jealous rage, changed Callisto into a bear. When Callisto died, she was placed in the sky as the constellation of Ursa Major, or the Great Bear.

The number of Greek myths is truly astonishing, and those about nymphs make up a large portion. Two gods of the sea, Okeanos and Nereus, between them had quantities of nymph daughters. Okeanos had three thousand daughters (the Okeanids), and Nereus had fifty sons (the Tritons) and fifty daughters (the Nereids).

One Nereid, Amphitrite, became queen of the sea by marrying Poseidon. He first saw her dancing with her sisters on the island of Naxos and asked her to marry him. At first she refused and ran away to seek the protection of the giant Atlas. Poseidon sent a dolphin, who found her hiding place and brought her back to the god. The dolphin was rewarded by a place in the sky as a constellation. Amphitrite consented to marry Poseidon and they had three children, a son and two daughters. One, Rhode, has given her name to the island of Rhodes.

Fortunately, Amphitrite was not often jealous, for Poseidon was almost constantly in love with some goddess or nymph. But a nymph named Scylla, whom Poseidon loved, did arouse Amphitrite's jealousy, perhaps because she was unusually beautiful. Amphitrite threw poisonous herbs into a pool where Scylla bathed and turned her into a hideous monster with six heads, each with a triple row of teeth. Thereafter, Scylla dwelt in a cave by the sea, snatching one man from the crew of every ship that passed close enough for her to reach.

Scylla was a personification of one of the twin dangers—a high

The sea nymph Thetis, mother of Achilles, with her dolphins. From a Greek plate which was painted about 500 B.C.

71

This silver coin of Syracuse in Sicily portrays the nymph Arethusa. It is a famous Greek coin, dated 479 B.C.

rock on one hand and a whirlpool on the other—that threatened mariners at the Strait of Messina, between Sicily and Italy. Myths were often explanations of such puzzling natural phenomena. Another such story is about the nymph Echo, who was one of Hera's attendants. She distracted Hera with her chatter and singing so that the other nymphs could flirt with Zeus. When Hera discovered what Echo was doing, she condemned her to be able to speak only the last syllable of any phrase or word. This inability to speak intelligibly caused Narcissus, a young man with whom Echo was in love, to desert her. For this he was punished in his turn. He was made to love only his own image, so that he spent the rest of his life looking at his reflection in a pool.

Nymphs were often shadowy figures with little power, but a few were close to goddesses in importance. Thetis, a Nereid, was a well-known nymph. Both Zeus and Poseidon loved her, but since a prophecy said that she would have a son more powerful than his father, both gods thought it wiser to give her up. Zeus arranged a marriage for Thetis with a human king, Peleus. Their son was Achilles, the hero of the *Iliad*, for whom his mother often interceded with the gods.

Perhaps there are so many myths about nymphs because these lovely creatures charmed the mythmakers. They loved to depict these maiden deities, who forever remained young and beautiful.

72

ξ is for **ξεω**, or in English letters *xeo* (pronounced *xéh-oh*), to carve.

The Greek statues in our museums are pale reflections of those that ancient people saw. Their creators never intended statues to be white (or gray) as they are now. The Greeks painted both wood and marble sculpture with bright colors and adorned it with bronze, gold, ivory, and sometimes precious stones. Bronze statues were kept shining, and most of this brilliant and colorful sculpture was seen out of doors in the strong sunlight of Greece. Temples were rich with sculpture; fully founded figures in the hollow, triangular pediments at each end of the building over the columns, and bas-reliefs—figures only slightly detached from the wall—ran the length of each outside wall. Inside each temple stood an enormous statue of the god or goddess for whom it was built.

The *Zeus* at Olympia, by Phidias, was such a colossal statue. It was made of wood and was covered with sheets of ivory and sheets of gold, with precious stones for the eyes. The god was seated, wearing a golden cloak on which a pattern, like embroidery, was indicated in many colors. To the ancient people who came with offerings and

White marble statue of a harpist from the Cyclades Islands in the Aegean Sea. Cycladic statues were pre-Greek. This one dates from about 2500 B.C.

Greek statues were painted, and this scene (from a wine bowl) shows how it was done. Color was mixed with hot wax. The artist laid it on with a spatula, then burned it into the marble with a tool, heated by his assistant. Here the artist has just begun to paint a statue of Heracles. Zeus and a winged Victory watch over the scene. Left: A small bronze statue of the god Hermes in the manner of early Greek sculpture, which somewhat resembled the stiff Egyptian style. Hermes was the protector of flocks and travelers, here symbolized by the ram he holds and the hat and boots he wears prayers, this representation of Zeus, towering more than forty feet above them, was an awesome and moving sight. An early Greek traveler has described his feelings thus: "When you stand before this statue you forget every misfortune of our earthly life, even if you have been broken by adversities and grief." Zeus himself shared in the admiration of his statue. An urn stood in the same room, marking a spot hit by a bolt of lightning which, the ancients said, Zeus had sent to congratulate Phidias on his splendid piece of work.

Greek sculptors began, at a very early period, to do fine work in gold, silver, bronze, and clay. They seem to have turned to carving marble after seeing huge stone statues in Egypt. Early Greek marbles are stiff figures, all facing squarely to the front, with the face framed by long curls, markedly similar to Egyptian statues. But Greek craftsmen soon made these figures more alive and more lifelike. The Greeks introduced revolutionary changes to the art of sculpture. They were the first to carve nude statues and to show figures in motion. So well did the Greek sculptors master the many materials they used that they were able to honor their gods and beautify their cities with sculpture that was appropriately dignified and serene, but at the same time full of vigor and life.

The work of the Greek sculptors who were most famous in their

Marble statue of a Greek youth in the Egyptian style. These stiff figures of youths were called kouroi. Later Greek sculpture was more lifelike

75

This head of a goddess was found in Taranto, Italy. It is typical of the big marble sculptures made in Greece during the fifth century. The holes in the head were meant to hold a crown and earrings, like the ornaments shown here. The intricate gold earring of Victory in a chariot was far too large to be worn by any ordinary woman. So was the gold wreath

own time has been almost entirely lost. Phidias was often called the greatest, but we know of his *Zeus* at Olympia and his equally colossal *Athena* at Athens only from drawings, reproductions on coins, and the descriptions of ancient writers. Some of the finest of Greek marble sculpture is in London. Known as "the Elgin Marbles" (after Lord Elgin, who brought them to England) they originally adorned the Parthenon, the temple to Athena in Athens. The Parthenon sculpture was done under the supervision of Phidias and so must reflect his style, and some may possibly be by his own hand.

Praxiteles, a later sculptor almost as much praised as Phidias, is known to us chiefly by reputation. His only remaining statue is one of the god Hermes, and it is possible that it is a copy, not an original. Two other sculptors, Myron and Lysippus, had great reputations, but their sculpture has entirely disappeared. A statue of a discus thrower by Myron is well known from copies. The Athenians greatly enjoyed a cow by Myron, which was said to be so true to life that dogs barked at it and calves tried to suckle it.

The Romans were passionate admirers of Greek sculpture and transported vast quantities of marbles and bronzes to Italy. The emperor Nero took five hundred statues from Delphi at one time, and Sulla, the Roman general who burned and looted Athens, carried off twelve hundred ships of booty, consisting of libraries and works of art. In Rome, every rich man wanted to have a garden full of Greek statuary. The result was that factories were set up to turn out copies of the originals, and eventually they were producing copies of copies of copies. Many of these are in museums today, and no one can be sure how truly they represent the spirit of the original Greek works.

Greek sculpture made a tremendous impact on artists of later times, who studied and copied it, so that we accept as normal much that was daring and new in Greek days. The Greeks had a saying (modesty was not one of their virtues): "Whatever the Greeks inherit from other peoples, in the end they turn it into something better." This was undoubtedly true in the field of sculpture, and one art critic, Charles Seltman, has said, "There can be no doubt that the meeting of Greek and Egyptian art . . . was one of the greatest events in the art history of the world."

O

o is for **οικουρος**, or in English letters
oikouros (pronounced *oy-koo-róss*), a housewife.

The ancient Greek housewife cared for her children, cooked the meals, and kept her house—her *oikos*—clean and in order. But living in ancient Greece, she had a great deal more to do, including jobs that required special skills and training. Almost every item of food, clothing, and bedding used by the family was prepared or made in the house. The *oikouros* needed help with the many crafts she engaged in, and often she had slaves, but she expected her daughters to do their share. Girls did not go to school like their brothers, but were taught by their mothers all of the household skills, and occasionally, also, music and reading and writing.

In a Greek house the women and girls spent much of their time in

A small boy takes a shower at the public fountain where the women come to fill the beautiful household jugs which they carry away on their heads. Such jugs were often painted with scenes like these

a courtyard, which was the center of family life. It was open to the sky and often planted with fruit trees and flowers. The housewife could watch the small children, who played there most of the day. In the morning, after she had helped the boys get off to school at the same early hour at which the men departed, the *oikouros* assigned the various jobs to her helpers.

Before bread could be baked or porridge made, the grain had to be ground into flour. This was done by hand in a stone bowl with a stone pestle and was a long, tiresome job which usually fell to the lot of slave girls. They, too, were the ones sent with huge jugs to the public fountain for water, because it was not considered proper for the girls and women of the family to go out on the city streets.

The most skilled work that a Greek mother taught her daughters were the handicrafts involved in making cloth. Cloth was usually wool, though some rich families also made linen. When a bundle of fleece, just sheared from the sheep, was left in the courtyard, the women had to know all the processes that would transform it into fine dresses, men's cloaks, or blankets.

First the fleece was washed and then it was carded, a combing process that made the wool soft and fluffy and ready to be spun into yarn. If linen was made, the housewife softened flax plants till they

Three thousand years ago, a mother was shown playing with her baby who is seated in a very substantial Greek high chair

80

These small terra-cotta figures, from the
fifth century B.C., show women at their
household tasks. One rolls the dough,
after having spent hours grinding the
grain into flour. Another is grating
cheese into a dish. A third shows her
little girl what's cooking in the pot

Scenes taken from the painting on an oil jar, photographed on the facing page Two weavers are shown working at the upright Greek loom. The woman with the basket is preparing wool for the spinner who holds her distaff high, while the weighted spindle twists the thread. In the photo, two women fold the cloth

could be spun into linen thread. Dyeing was done either before or after spinning. A favorite color was a reddish purple made from whelks, sea snails that were shipped from the Phoenician city of Tyre. After spinning came the weaving of the fabric. The weavers moved back and forth for long hours in front of the tall looms, and the girls watched how the women slipped the bright yarn through the upright threads.

A typically Greek art that girls were taught was that of making wreaths. Thyme, myrtle, ivy, parsley, and laurel were the plants most used. A fresh wreath was put daily on the altar of Hestia, the goddess of the household, and many houses had at the door a figure of the god Hermes, which was similarly adorned. A father inviting his friends in for the evening would expect his daughters to make a garland for each man to wear on his head at the party. An infrequent but exciting need for many wreaths was for the marchers in the processions of the festivals. Excursions outside of the house were rare treats for girls—and for housewives, too—but they took part in the festivals of their city. A group of girls always led the procession of the greatest Athenian festival, the Panathenaea. Another festival held in Athens every spring, to honor the god Dionysus, consisted largely of theatrical performances. Women and girls attended the theater for three or four successive days during this festival.

82

But most days of the year a girl stayed at home, learning to be an *oikouros*—to spin and weave and cook and sew. She hoped to have laid away in a perfumed chest a supply of garments and bedding by the time she would marry—at the age of thirteen or fourteen, although the bridegroom was usually a good deal older. If she was a clever needle-worker, a girl added embroidery to much of her handiwork. At Athens there was particular excitement connected with embroidery. At the special Panathenaea that took place every fourth year the most expert embroiderers decorated a robe, woven of saffron-colored wool, large enough for the forty-foot statue of Athena. In the procession which wound up onto the Acropolis the robe hung from the yardarm of a ship mounted on rollers and pushed by young men. That the presentation of the robe was the climax of the festival served as public recognition of the skill of women's work.

Greek women have often been described as uneducated, playing no part in society. But Greek literature includes bloody Clytemnestra, Helen, for whom a nine years' war was fought; goddesses like wise and warlike Athena; and the huntress Artemis. It is hard to imagine such characters created in a land where the real women were weak and retiring.

83

Π π is for **Παρθενων**, or in English letters *Parthenon* (pronounced *par-then-óhn*), the Parthenon.

The word Parthenon means "a maiden's room." It is a modest name for the temple at Athens which ancient peoples considered the most perfect building in the world. It was a temple for Athena, who was called the maiden goddess and who was the patron and protector of Athens. The Parthenon was built of gleaming white marble, now weathered to a golden honey color. It stands high on the Acropolis, visible from the whole city and a wide area beyond. It rises above the city like a symbol of the greatness of Athens in the fifth century B.C., when she led all of Hellas in arts and literature and wealth.

This great period of Athenian life was the time of her democracy, and the building of the Parthenon was part of the democratic way of life that the Greeks called the *polis*. Greek cities lavished their money and artistic talents on public buildings—on temples above all—that belonged to all of the citizens. Private houses in Greece were simple and

84

unpretentious. After the almost prehistoric period of the Mycenaean kings the Greeks built no palaces or luxurious homes for rulers or powerful men. The temple, which honored both a god and a city, and the theaters, where the whole population flocked to see performances that were partly religious, became the contributions of the Greeks to architecture.

Temple architecture was not invented in Greece. There were columned temples in Egypt and in Asia Minor. The Greeks, however, added new features and refined this art, giving it a distinctive style. They perfected three types of columns, called the three orders, which are seen today on buildings in many countries. The Parthenon architects used the Doric column, the strongest and simplest of the three. The taller and slimmer Ionic column is the most graceful, with a capital at its top in the form of two opposing curves like coiled ram's horns. The third type, invented by the Greeks but little used by them, was employed extensively by the Romans. This is the Corinthian column, with a capital of stylized acanthus leaves.

When it was found on the Acropolis in 1864 this life-size marble statue still showed traces of its original blue paint. It was probably given to the temple by a wealthy Greek citizen about 570 B.C.

85

The ruined Parthenon, as it appears today, is shown in this photograph. Some idea of what it looked like in the fifth century B.C. is seen in the drawing at the left. It dominated the top of the Acropolis, which was crowded with smaller temples and painted statuary. Inside the Parthenon stood a magnificent 40-foot statue of the goddess Athena, made of gold and ivory. It was the work of the great Greek sculptor Phidias. Not even a fragment of the Athena remains today, but some idea of its majesty can be seen in the drawing above, taken from a Roman copy

The way in which the Parthenon was built gives an interesting sidelight on Athenian democracy. The great monuments of most countries of the ancient world were built exclusively by huge gangs of slaves. But the Athenian temple was built by the citizens themselves together with slaves. It was a community project involving many citizens, each contracting to do a certain small portion of the work. One was paid to bring so many loads of marble from the nearby quarry, employing one or two other citizens and using several slaves and one ox; another took charge of erecting and fluting one column. Foreigners, too, who could not be citizens in Athens, worked beside the slaves and citizens at the same jobs, many of which took a high degree of skill. The marble pieces, for example, were fitted without mortar, but so skillfully that even today it is difficult to see where they join.

All phases of the construction of the Parthenon were under the direction of the sculptor Phidias. He was chosen, as were the architects, Ictinus and Callicrates, by the great statesman Pericles, who was leading the government of Athens. Pericles planned the Parthenon as part of the rebuilding of the city after its destruction in 480 B.C. by the Persians. The temple was begun in 447 B.C., and by 438 it was near enough to completion for the installation and dedication of the huge statue of Athena that stood in one of its two rooms.

Three sections from the Parthenon frieze which depicted the procession of the Panathenaea. The entire frieze ran for 524 feet along the outer walls of the temple.behind the great columns. These fragments are among the outstanding examples which remain of Greek sculpture at its height. The overall design of the frieze was said to have been made by Phidias, but many anonymous sculptors worked for years to create this masterpiece

From the time it was built the Parthenon has been universally admired, and it has often been called the greatest architectural masterpiece in the world. The temple, with columns on all four sides, was designed with simple, harmonious lines, meant to be impressive from a distance. It was richly decorated with sculpture, much of which told stories of Athena. On the east end was a scene of her birth, and on the opposite end she was shown in battle with Poseidon for possession of Attica, the region surrounding Athens.

A bas-relief frieze ran around the entire temple, high up on the outside walls. It showed the procession of the Panathenaea, in which a group of seated gods awaits the procession which is approaching them, headed by a group of girls. Following the girls are young men on prancing horses, priests leading animals to be sacrificed, and young people carrying jugs of wine, fruit, and other offerings for the goddess. There are pipers and musicians playing stringed instruments, quantities of marching people, and some rich men or dignitaries riding in chariots. Finally, Athena's robe, now folded, is being presented to a priest. Part of the Parthenon's sculpture was removed by Lord Elgin in 1806 and taken to England, where it now rests in the British Museum.

There were amazing methods used in the construction of the Parthenon. By subtle mathematical calculations, the architects curved every apparently straight line. The base on which the columns stand bows up slightly in the center. Each column bulges in the middle and tapers toward the top, and the two end columns of each row tip slightly inward. These devices are based on the way the human eye sees lines at a distance. The lines *look* straight, but its designers knew that these slight, carefully planned curves saved the building from having a heavy or dull look, and gave it a lively, graceful appearance.

The Romans, who were great engineers, both admired and were puzzled by these engineering feats, which they knew involved great expenditures of time and work. They did not share a Greek aspiration called *arete*, which was the achievement of excellence in any pursuit, no matter what the cost. If it were possible to improve the looks of the temple, even slightly, the Greeks felt that any amount of time, money, and effort was well spent.

The reactions of viewers through the ages prove how successful the architects were. Plutarch, in the first century A.D., speaks of the temple's "freshness and vigor" and its "youthful gayety." A modern writer, Robert Payne, says of the building, even in its present half-ruined state, "there is something almost insolent in the way the Parthenon says quietly: 'I have been worn to the bone, but I am the most living of all things.'"

P

ρ is for **ρʿαψωδος**, or in English letters *rhapsodos* (pronounced *rap-soh-dóss*), a bard.

A bard made his living by traveling about, reciting the poems of Homer at festivals and other large public gatherings. Listening to bards or minstrels recite poetry was a favorite recreation of the ancient Greeks. Even before Homer's time such bards entertained the pirate kings and their nobles by chanting old tales to a lyre accompaniment. Odysseus speaks of it in the *Odyssey*:

> *How beautiful it is to hear a minstrel,*
> *like a god as he sings.*
> *When banqueters listen to a harpist*
> *in a great hall beside the tables heaped*
> *with bread and roasted meat,*
> *it seems to me this is the best thing there is.*

Drawing of a rhapsodos, *one of the skilled performers who recited Homer's poems at Greek festivals. He holds a staff, called a* rabdos, *symbol of his professional skill*

91

Odysseus speaks of the bard as having "the skill to shape his song," and the word *rhapsodos* means "one who stitches odes." These are good descriptions of the way the earliest minstrels put together an evening's selection out of a great store of traditional tales, passages, and oft-repeated sentences. Later, in the democratic states, the *rhapsodos* was a performer who did not put together the poetry but recited a fixed text. This text was usually Homer, and it no longer had musical accompaniment. In Athens, laws regulated the performances at the Pana-thenaea, stating that only Homer's poems were to be presented. They had to be done in their entirety and in correct order, one *rhapsodos* following another like relay racers.

A *rhapsodos* had to be a skillful performer, for every one of his listeners knew the tales he told. He had a highly responsive audience, however. Plato describes a bard named Ion, who said: " 'Whenever I speak of sad and touching scenes, my eyes are full of tears; when it is something terrible or awful, my hair stands up straight with fear and my heart leaps! . . . I always look down from my platform, and there they are crying and glaring and amazed, according to what I say.' "

Homer himself was one of the very early minstrels who "stitched" his poems out of legends of the gods and ancient heroes. He may have been blind, as tradition says, and as minstrels often were. He probably

92

came from the coast of Asia Minor or one of the islands near it, and in this area many cities have claimed his birthplace. But little is known of this poet, who has been said to have "no superior, perhaps no equal, in all the poetry that has followed."

The fact that Homer's poems were to be heard and not read explains much about their style. The story moves swiftly, with many vivid details, and can easily be grasped at the first hearing. When a guest arrives in a Homeric poem, we are told just how he crossed the threshold, who brought him a silver basin to wash his hands, who gave him a cup of wine to slake his thirst, and so on. Homer expressed a typically Greek enjoyment in even the smallest events of life.

It has been said that Homer gave the Greeks three things: their language, their gods, and their unity. Obviously, one man could not actually do all of this, but it is easy to see why it has been said. Homer composed his poems in the Dark Ages, when the separate Greek tribes were just beginning to form one Hellenic people. The tribes spoke different Greek dialects, and it was Homer who first gave them a literary language, which later writers used as a standard. Secondly, the Greeks turned to the *Iliad* and the *Odyssey* with a special eagerness because the poems told them so much about their gods. The accounts by Homer of the Olympians and of the earliest Greek heroes and wars provided

The dead Patroclus, friend of Achilles, is carried from the field of battle. The Greek potter-painters often depicted scenes from the Iliad *and the* Odyssey. *This is from the François Vase, 570 B.C.*

Another Homeric scene shows Odysseus escaping from the cave of Polyphemus by clinging to one of the giant's sheep

a common heritage for all Hellenes, who were otherwise so separated by geography and often at war with one another. Thirdly, Homer continued to be a unifying influence even long after his death, because from the earliest Greek schools to the present day his poems have been studied and many passages memorized by Greek children.

Poets of later times in other countries were much influenced by Homer, and have paid him many tributes. Shelley for instance, says that Homer "excelled Shakespeare." An earlier personage who honored Homer, but not in words, was Alexander the Great. In the midst of his conquests, he made a stop at Troy and sought out the tomb of Achilles, hero of the *Iliad*. He paid homage to the great warrior by pouring a libation; then, stripping off his clothes, the better to show respect, he ran naked three times around Achilles's tomb.

Σ σ is for $\Sigma\pi\alpha\rho\tau\eta$, or in English letters *Sparte* (pronounced *spár-tay*), Sparta.

The city of Sparta was said to look like an overgrown army camp. It did not have temples, theaters, beautiful statues, gardens, or an *agora*, as did other Greek cities. Nor did it have a harbor busy with traffic in grain, olive oil, pottery, and other products of expert craftsmen. The Spartan citizenry did not include craftsmen, painters, sculptors, architects, poets, or dramatists.

At one time Sparta had all of these typically Hellenic characteristics. But in the seventh century B.C. she turned to a different and strange way of life. At that time the Spartans conquered Lacedaemonia, a large area of the Peloponnese, the southern part of Greece, in which their city was located. The conquered people became serfs,

This bronze statuette, though only some four inches high, manages to convey the grimness and power of a Spartan soldier

called helots, who worked the soil for the benefit of their rulers. The Spartans (also called Lacedaemonians) continued with their conquests until they had the largest state in ancient Greece. The Spartans themselves, the citizens, were fewer in number than those of almost any other city-state.

A serious revolt of the helots persuaded the Spartans that they must subordinate everything to becoming the strongest possible military state if they were to keep their workers under control. Arts, literature, any form of handicraft, and the handling of money were banned for citizens. Seafaring was also forbidden, but the Spartans had a large and fertile territory so that they did not need to import food, and they desired so few goods that they had no need of foreign trade. In short, a Spartan was to be a ruler and a soldier and nothing else.

The children were trained for this way of life from the beginning. Those who appeared weak or deformed were abandoned at birth on lonely mountainsides. The rest were brought up by their mothers until the boys were seven years old, when they moved into barracks. Spartan men lived in barracks until they were thirty. The boys learned to read and were taught music, but most of their training was aimed at toughening them physically. Their food was scanty, but Greeks of other cities joked that it was remarkable that Spartans ate as much as they did,

Warfare was the chief occupation of a Spartan citizen.
This scene shows Greek foot soldiers, equipped with
spears and enormous, decorated shields. It is taken from
the painting on a large bowl, shown on the right

considering the coarseness of the fare they were given. Boys wore one garment and no shoes or sandals, winter and summer. Girls were given rigorous training in sports so that they would be healthy mothers.

The state maintained secret police, and boys were taught to spy so that they could discover any signs of revolt among their subject people. The helots could not be sold like slaves, but were not allowed to move from their land, where they were forced to grow the crops that fed the Spartans. There was another large class of conquered people, the *perioikoi*, with whom the Lacedaemonians never mingled. These were the artisans, the carpenters, armor makers, painters, and builders. The *perioikoi* performed all the jobs that were forbidden to the ruling class.

The Spartan system succeeded in producing brave and completely disciplined soldiers, who even gave up the right to think for themselves—the right so treasured by most Greeks. On the monument at Thermopylae, where a band of Spartans died fighting the Persian invaders, is a moving inscription that well expresses their ideal of bravery and perfect obedience:

> *Stranger, tell the men of Lacedaemon:*
> *We who lie buried here*
> *did what they told us to do.*

The Spartan way of life discouraged innovation, and it continued unchanged for centuries. The women entered into its stern spirit. They felt it their mission to bring up sons to be brave soldiers in the service of the state. The tale is often told of a Spartan mother who admonished her son, who was going out to fight, to return "with his shield or upon it." Dead soldiers were carried on the huge shields, and the loss of his shield was considered a sign that the soldier had been a coward and run away from battle.

Archilochus, a poet from Paros, illustrates the light-hearted attitude of Greeks of other cities, which contrasted sharply with the grim Spartan ideal. Archilochus was not in the least prepared to risk his life for his shield:

> Some Thracian glories in my shield
> that I left underneath a bush.
> Too bad I left that good shield there,
> but I, myself, escaped from death.
> So never mind the shield. I'll
> get another one no worse.

A Greek warrior leaving for battle. He is fully equipped with shield, spears, greaves for his legs, and a great helmet

99

T τ is for $\tau\epsilon\chi\nu\eta$, or in English letters *techne* (pronounced *ték-nay*), art.

Techne also means the skill and the rules, or technique, by which a work of art is created.

Not all Greek works of art were monumental like the temples and statues. Many were in humbler mediums, for Greek craftsmen made art of whatever they turned their hands to, including all the objects used in the house. Painters spread lively scenes on plates, jugs, pitchers, pots, cups, and bowls. They made drawings even on the little perfume bottles and cosmetic jars that ladies used, as well as on the enormous, graceful jars in which grain, oil, and wine were shipped throughout the Hellenic world.

The orange-and-black paintings that appear on household pottery are of clear figures, standing out starkly against an empty background. The essence of a person or a scene seems to be abstracted by the artist with a sure line. All Greek artists were concerned with human beings, or with gods and goddesses and nymphs, who were indistinguishable in looks from human beings. The people seem larger than life-size and are idealized figures, not portraits of particular individuals. This Hellenic style runs through all the Greek arts, even poetry and literature, and appeared in all the widely scattered Greek cities.

From the early Mycenaean days, Greek artists who worked in metal designed handsome gold and silver bowls and cups. These were often beautifully embossed, as was bronze armor if the man paying for it were rich enough. Thus, metal craftsmen, too, expended their talents on useful objects. Greek ladies wore delicate gold jewelry, especially earrings, necklaces, and diadems. Statues were adorned with jewels, which were huge, in keeping with the colossal gods and goddesses. Parts of Greek jewelry were often hung on fine wires so that they moved and gave a shimmering effect.

The Greeks developed the use of coins, and cities vied with one another in the artistry with which they stamped silver pieces. Sculptors worked also in an even smaller medium, engraving and carving gems with exquisite designs to make seals used by businessmen as signatures when they could not write. On both seals and coins appeared mythological creatures—from griffons to Pegasus—and also bulls, horses, deer, goats, lions, dolphins, cranes, and other birds, as well as the human heroes whom cities wished to commemorate.

Greek craftsmanship (techne) is revealed in this impressive figure of Zeus in a splendidly embroidered robe, seated on an ornate chair intricately carved with a dog and bird's head. From a painted cup

101

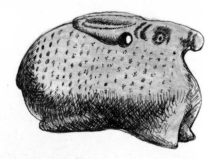

The Greek potter gave artistry to household objects. Here is a baby's nursing bottle in the shape of a mouse, a perfume flask in the form of a rabbit, and a fine wine cup. The drawing on the left shows an artisan working on the decoration of a large, ornate pottery bowl

We have to judge all of the Greek arts by what remains, and this may give us a one-sided or unfair picture, depending, as it does, on chance and the durability of the materials. Murals on the walls of public buildings were the paintings most praised by the Greeks themselves. But we know almost nothing about them, for they have not survived the hazards of time. However, many pictures done in mosaics on floors have survived, because of the hard materials used—sea-washed pebbles or tiny squares of colored clay tile. These mosaic floors portrayed informal and delightful scenes. Embroidery, too, was considered a fine art; one writer has even described Zeus spending his time at this craft. It is remarkable that even a few tiny pieces of Greek embroidered fabrics are still in existence. They are in a museum in Leningrad in the Soviet Union, and were found in Mongolia, in central Asia.

Greek art traveled great distances—much farther than the Greeks themselves. The reputation of Greek craftsmen was so great that their work was sought after by kings and wealthy men of other lands, who bought them for special gifts or prizes. Pieces of Greek jewelry have been found at the headwaters of the Nile, which rises over four thousand miles from the Mediterranean. And a few years ago a remarkably fine Greek bronze bowl, six feet high, was found near Paris in the tomb of a Celtic princess. Much Greek art found a home in Rome. The

Romans were the first to collect and display as art Greek household dishes, cups, jars, coins, seals, and jewelry.

Since ancient times the products of Greek artists have traveled across oceans to countries, and even to continents, that the Greeks did not know existed. There, in museums, an earring of a great lady, a Greek businessman's seal engraved with a prancing horse, or a fine bowl presented to a winning athlete are close by the pots and jugs once used in humble Greek kitchens. All these things are united by the *techne* of the craftsmen, which transformed them from items intended for everyday use into objects that are displayed as treasures thousands of years later.

Two beautiful examples of carved gems, the smallest medium for Greek techne. Such stones were exquisitely detailed and were often signed by the gem cutter

Y υ is for υ῾ποκριτης, or in English letters *hupokrites* (pronounced *hoo-pok-rit-áce*), an actor.

Most of our theatrical words—theater, tragedy, comedy, orchestra, and others—come from ancient Greece, because the art of the theater began there. The meanings of some words have changed. For instance, to the Greeks *hupokrites* meant an actor on the stage, but the English "hypocrite" means one who plays his false role in real life.

"Drama" is the same in the two languages, but a performance of a drama in ancient Greece was on a scale that has never been equaled anywhere since. The plays were presented in huge outdoor amphitheaters before thousands of people. In Athens, where drama began, most of the population of the city would be there: men, women, children, foreigners, and even some slaves. Every spring, at festival time, they

Greek actor, holding a mask, and dressed in the costume of an Oriental king

105

came at dawn each day and sat on hard, backless benches till dusk to watch the tragedies and comedies. These performances continued for three or four days. The huge holiday audience sat enthralled, because the plays were about their gods and their heroes, and touched them deeply.

Greek drama developed out of a spring festival that was a favorite with the country people who had celebrated it from the earliest days of Greek history. This festival was in honor of Dionysus, the god of wine and revelry, and in the fifth century B.C. it became one of the greatest of Athenian celebrations. A central part of the ritual was a long narrative poem, or ode, that was sung by a large chorus. In 534 B.C. a playwright named Thespis took the first step that changed this choral ode into a play. He introduced an actor—a *hupokrites*—to engage in dialogue with the leader of the chorus.

About fifty years later, Aeschylus, the first of the great Athenian dramatists, added a second actor, and true theater had begun. Sophocles, his successor, added a third, but the number of actors in Greek plays always remained small. The chorus never ceased to play an important role, singing or chanting many of the verses, and dancing in a circular area called the *orchestra*—which in the Greek language means "a dancing place."

Part of the chorus in a Greek comedy. A flute player leads the dance. The male dancers are costumed as horses and riders. Music and dance were important in all Greek plays

Masks like these were worn by Greek actors to symbolize the roles they played

Greek plays, though presented before the whole population, were not at all what we today consider "popular" entertainment. The comedies, it is true, were full of slapstick and horseplay and by modern standards were very ribald. But the larger number of plays were tragedies, and these were written in complicated verse forms and dealt with lofty and abstract subjects, such as the role of fate in men's lives, or the punishment of arrogance by the gods. These tragedies were full of bloody deeds and grim events, and the characters were symbols as well as people. For instance, at the terrible climax of Sophocles's play *Agamemnon,* the heroic king is stabbed by his wife, Clytemnestra. This crime represented more than a particular wife killing her husband. It represented also the working out of fate, and the inevitability of retribution for a deed long past.

The fifth century Athenian audience responded passionately to these plays, according to Greek writers of the times. One writer tells of a terrible scene on the stage which caused many women and children to faint. At times the applause was tumultuous, and at other times there were storms of hisses. Actors were sometimes held responsible for the deeds they enacted and were pelted with rotten fruit, and once an actor was stoned almost to death.

Aeschylus was the most abstract of the three great tragedians. He explored religious subjects, especially the relations of the gods with men. Sophocles was less involved with these theoretical subjects and more interested in his human characters, but his people remained aloof and impersonal figures, whether splendid or tragic. Euripides, the last great writer of tragedies, was concerned with people's feelings and gave his characters normal human weaknesses. This caused contemporary critics to call him irreverent and revolutionary. The fourth great figure in Athenian drama was Aristophanes, a writer of comedies. He portrayed everyday life in Athens, making fun (often savagely) of politicians, other writers, public officials, and even the gods. Serious criticism, bawdy fun, and occasional lovely poetic lyrics are mingled in his plays.

These were the playwrights who year after year won the first prizes at the festivals and were most admired by their contemporaries. There were many other Greek dramatists, but their work has been entirely lost. The Greeks called the writers of plays "poets," but they had a great many other functions besides writing. They were in charge of all phases of the production and thus had to be composers, choreographers, directors, producers, and sometimes scenery and costume designers. The costumes for the comedies were grotesque, heavily padded on the abdomen and on the buttocks, and often had tails attached. The

Clytemnestra, wielding a double ax, is shown in this detail from a painted bowl. The tragic story of Agamemnon and his queen, Clytemnestra, was a favorite subject of Greek dramatists and artists

109

actors of both comedy and tragedy wore masks, which sometimes had megaphones inside to amplify their voices, although the acoustics of the ancient amphitheaters were remarkably good. Tragic actors also wore shoes with high, built-up soles to add to their stature. These and the masks contributed to making the characters seem symbolic and impersonal.

The plays performed at the festival of Dionysus were written by the winners of a contest for playwrights. Each of the three winners was assigned one day on which he presented three tragedies in the morning and a comic play in the afternoon. At the end of the festival the best playwright received a much-coveted first prize. Throughout all of the fifth century and into the middle of the fourth, the fame of this contest at Athens was so great that dramatists from all parts of the Greek world came there to compete.

Only after Athens had lost her dominating position in Greek life and her civilization had fallen into decline were theaters built in many other Hellenic cities. Then the famous plays written for the Athenian contest and performed only once in the theater of Dionysus began to be presented in other places. New plays were also presented in these later times, but none could compete in quality with the works of the great Athenian dramatists.

Φ φ is for **φιλοσοφια**, or in English letters *philosophia* (pronounced *phil-oh-soph-eé-ah*), philosophy.

Socrates, Plato, and Aristotle were the greatest philosophers of the ancient world, and no other Greeks have made such an impact on later ages. They concerned themselves with the same questions that philosophers have explored ever since. What is the purpose of the world? What is a good man? Does a good society make good men, or good men a good society? Philosophers of the present day pursue these questions in classrooms, libraries, and studies full of books and papers. The Greek philosophers pursued the same problems in gymnasiums. A Greek "gymnasium" was a large tract of land containing groves of trees, gardens full of statues, colonnaded walks, and sometimes small theaters,

This might be a philosophical discussion at a Greek gymnasium. The scene is taken from a painting by Douris, a much-admired potter in the fifth century B.C.

111

as well as racetracks, stadia, and public baths. There the philosophers walked and talked with their students and associates.

Socrates spent all of the daylight hours of his adult life either in a gymnasium or on the streets of Athens and the *agora*. In the evening he often continued to talk at a friend's house, sometimes till dawn of the following day. He was a familiar sight to all Athenians, a short man with a big belly, a small button nose, and a gait described as a waddle. He scorned money and worldly possessions. Socrates's method of pursuing philosophy was to ask questions. His seemingly simple and innocent questions trapped his pupils into examining their beliefs. He turned philosophy toward ethics, the study of human behavior. Socrates lived in the great days of Athenian democracy and on into the beginning of its decline. He was particularly concerned with the *polis*, and he frequently discussed with his pupil Plato what made a perfect state.

Socrates, about forty years older than Plato, was seventy in 399 B.C., the year of his death. He had lived into the period of the war between Athens and Sparta and the time of a plague that wiped out much of the Athenian population. Perhaps these events contributed to the growing mood of suspicion and fear of new philosophies—a mood unusual in Athens, where respect for freedom of speech and thought had

112

been the rule. In any case, Socrates was accused of corrupting the young by teaching them of new divinities, and he was condemned to die by drinking a cup of hemlock, a poisonous drink.

No one mourned for Socrates more than his devoted follower Plato. But the two men had often disagreed, and the philosophy taught by Plato was very different from that of his master. It, too, was concerned with human conduct, but Plato scorned the democratic *polis* that Socrates admired. Plato wrote about an ideal state that would be run by the few best-educated and most intelligent men. One of his best-known theories was that there is a world of the mind, of ideas, superior to that of the physical world.

Plato wrote his books in the form of dialogues or conversations, with Socrates as the principal character. It is from Plato alone that we know what Socrates taught, for he himself wrote down nothing.

Aristotle, who lived from 384 to 322 B.C., was a pupil of Plato. Most of his life was spent at Athens, but it was a very different Athens from that which Plato and Socrates had known, and before Aristotle's death it was under the rule of Macedon. Aristotle studied with Plato when he was young, and then went to Macedon to be a tutor to young Alexander. Later he returned to Athens and taught philosophy. He taught ethics and politics like his two great predecessors, but he also

Socrates. This Roman copy of a Greek statuette closely fits his description

113

made important contributions in subjects they never touched. Aristotle did work that laid the foundation for several major sciences. He inaugurated a truly scientific method of study, making observations of plants and animals and carefully recording his findings. He was able to carry on this work on a large scale with the help of between four hundred and a thousand students, aided by money from Alexander the Great. This scientific work that Aristotle directed marked the beginnings of zoology, biology, and botany.

Aristotle evidently taught in the places and in the manner used by Socrates and Plato, because his followers were known as the Peripatetics, which means "those who walk around." By Aristotle's time, in the fourth century B.C.—and also in the third and second centuries B.C. —Greek philosophers made up many schools and groups. The names of these groups are often familiar to us, but usually in an oddly different way from their original meanings. The name of the Stoics, for example, did not mean indifference to pain, but a painted porch—a *stoa poikile*—where their leader, Zeno, held forth. The Epicureans, whose name now suggests luxury-loving, actually scorned any type of luxury, as did the Stoics. Both groups would have felt that their importance had nothing to do with luxury, one way or the other; their aim was to turn men's minds away from superstitions toward more rational ways of thinking.

The men who were truly "stoic" in doing without even the most modest aids to good living were the Cynics. Their name comes from the Greek word for "dog," because people felt that they existed like animals. Their leader, Diogenes, tried to live so closely to nature that he was said to eat his food raw and to sleep in a tub.

The influence of the Greek philosophers is hard to exaggerate. Their ideas dominated the Aegean and Near Eastern world at the time that Christianity was taking shape, and had a profound influence on Christian doctrine. (The New Testament was written in Greek.) During the Middle Ages, Aristotle was greatly admired, but in more recent times, many have considered Plato the master philosopher. Alfred North Whitehead, a twentieth century English philosopher, said that all European philosophy consists of "footnotes" on Plato. And Ralph Waldo Emerson, an earlier American philosopher, said that "the writings of Plato have preoccupied every school of learning, every lover of thought, every church poet,—making it impossible to think, on certain levels, except through him."

Two Greeks, seated in the marketplace (agora), debating a philosophical point, while a goose wanders by. Their cloaks hang on the wall behind them

Greek blacksmith, working on a helmet.
From a painted cup, fifth century B.C.

X χ is for **χαλκος**, or in English letters
chalkos (pronounced *kal-kóss*), bronze.

Bronze was the principal metal used by the Greeks of the Mycenaean
Age, also known as the Bronze Age. Later, when iron was the metal
most commonly used, *chalkos* became the name for iron, and in time
the word was used for metal in general. Our word "metal" comes from
the Greek *metallon*, "a mine," and the verb *metallao* means "to search."
This correctly suggests that in Greek lands mines and metals were
scarce and had to be searched for.

116

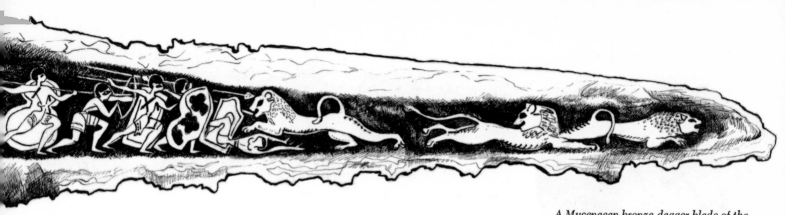

A Mycenaean bronze dagger blade of the 16th century B.C. The figures are inlaid in gold and silver. Time has eaten away the sharp edge but has not dulled the splendor of the workmanship

There were seven metals known to the ancient world: gold, silver, copper, tin, iron, lead, and mercury. The discovery that adding tin to copper made bronze, which was harder than either of its components, was made somewhere about 3000 B.C. The little Mycenaean kingdoms used bronze to make effective weapons. A man equipped with bronze arms and armor could easily dominate men armed only with sticks and stones. But copper was scarce in Greece, and tin even scarcer, so

117

that only the very rich could afford this luxury that gave them so much power. The Bronze Age was the only time in Greek life when kings and aristocrats had absolute rule over the people.

The Bronze Age was so early in recorded time that tools and implements had not begun to play an important part in people's lives. Although it could be used to make powerful weapons, bronze often seemed to the Greeks primarily valuable for its beauty, like gold and silver. The handsome appearance of armor delighted them, as is shown in a poem by a poet named Alcaeus:

> *The great house is all agleam with bronze.*
> *War has bedecked the whole roof with bright helmets,*
> *from which hang waving horse-hair plumes.*

He goes on to speak of bright bronze leg pieces, called greaves, stacked on the floor beside even larger piles of shields, made of leather covered with sheets of bronze.

It was *chalkos* (iron), brought by the Dorians about 1200 B.C., that made revolutionary changes in the Greek way of life. Iron ore was readily available, and working it was easy for local smiths once they had learned how to heat it in small furnaces, much like those long in

Producing iron tools in a Greek smithy. This drawing is taken from a painted oil jar of the sixth century B.C. It shows the kinds of tools made at that time

use for firing pottery. Farmers now had iron sickles, knives, axes, and spades with which to clear the land of trees and dig ditches for irrigation. Great new areas of land became usable for farming, and larger crops could be raised everywhere. The artisans in the cities increased their production with stronger and sharper tools, and built bigger ships more quickly with iron hammers and saws. Trade expanded, as did the population and prosperity of Greek cities. Warfare, too, became more deadly, with sharp, powerful swords and daggers now in the hands of many men.

The common man in Greece—the farmer, trader, artisan, and soldier—was no longer dependent for protection on a few bronze-armed aristocratic warriors. Iron played a large role in making possible the democratic period in Greek cities that succeeded the age of kings and nobles.

Another development in the use of metal sped up Greek life almost as much as the discovery of iron, and at about the same time. This was the use of coins, stamped with the symbol of the city issuing them, and guaranteeing a certain value. The Greeks got this idea, as they did many others, from Asia Minor. But the Greeks were the first people to make effective use of coinage. It made possible the great expansion of trade in all parts of the Mediterranean, in which many Greek cities took part. Aegina, Argos, Paros, and Corinth were cities that early began to issue silver coins. Athens having rich silver mines near the city, caught up with them later. In time, Athenian coins were the most valued and readily accepted in many lands.

Sparta, characteristically, never made beautiful silver coins, but used heavy, unadorned pieces of iron for money. But in all the other cities, coins, besides being such a vital part of commerce, became charming little works of art as well. Charles Seltman, an authority on ancient coins, has said of the Athenian *drachma*, which bears an owl, Athena's symbol, on one side and the goddess's head on the other: "The chubby, smiling goddess in the neat helmet, and the well-groomed, cocksure owl have a quality that is not surpassed in any other art."

A silver Athenian drachma. *The reverse side shows a head of Athena. This side shows an owl, symbol of Athena, and an olive spray, symbol of prosperity*

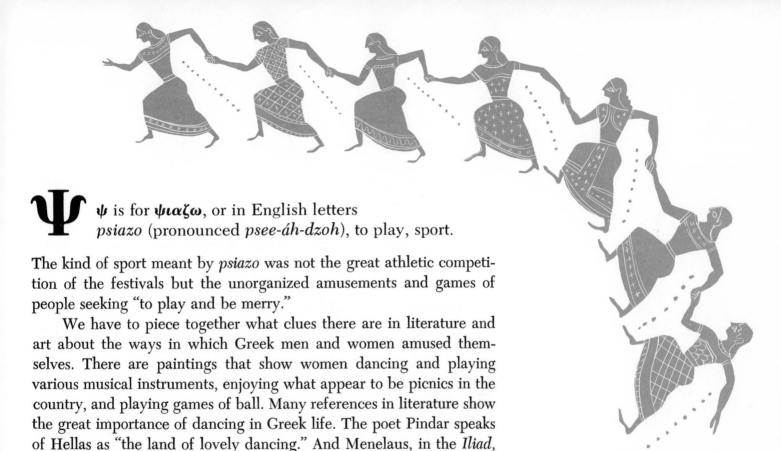

Ψ ψ is for **ψιαζω**, or in English letters
psiazo (pronounced *psee-áh-dzoh*), to play, sport.

The kind of sport meant by *psiazo* was not the great athletic competition of the festivals but the unorganized amusements and games of people seeking "to play and be merry."

We have to piece together what clues there are in literature and art about the ways in which Greek men and women amused themselves. There are paintings that show women dancing and playing various musical instruments, enjoying what appear to be picnics in the country, and playing games of ball. Many references in literature show the great importance of dancing in Greek life. The poet Pindar speaks of Hellas as "the land of lovely dancing." And Menelaus, in the *Iliad*, says that it is possible to have too much of anything, even "of sleep and love-making and sweet song and delightful dance."

Dancing women. From a painted cup, 570 B.C.

121

There is more evidence about the games and sports enjoyed by men than there is about those of women. The government set up public gymnasiums in Greek cities where men and boys could take part in all kinds of exercise and athletics. A favorite sport was hunting, which, when the land was still forested, gave the men the excitement and danger of killing big game—boars, wolves, bears, stags, and even lions. Later, when the forests had been cut down, the quarry was deer, rabbit, pheasant, thrushes, and other birds. Hunting a hare, according to one Greek writer, was so exciting that "it makes even a lover forget his heart's desire."

Another sport, so popular at Athens that it was held in huge amphitheaters, was cockfighting. The owners of the birds had a peculiar custom: when a cock was losing badly, its owner would snatch it up and shout directly into its ear so that it could not hear the triumphant crowing of its opponent and then be discouraged from continuing to fight.

Greek men made merry on many an evening at a kind of party called a symposium, which means, literally, "a drinking together." The guests had perhaps been invited to dinner, or had come in the evening after eating. The entertainment was varied, but the symposium was always governed by a set of rules like a game. One man was chosen as

The popular sports and games of ancient Greece were frequently the subjects of pottery painting. Here are a few examples: a handsome design showing a cockfight; a Greek boy playing with his dog; detail of a boar hunt, a favorite sport

a sort of chairman, and his first duty was to decide the proportion of water to be mixed with the wine and the amount of wine to be drunk. He chose the form of entertainment, which might be provided by girls who played on pipes and danced and sang. Or the men might entertain themselves by singing, or by telling stories or riddles, or by playing word games. In any case, each man took his turn as they sat in a circle, each with a garland on his head. In the homes of a few learned men, like the philosophers, there might be serious discussion of some scholarly subject. This explains the curious change in meaning that the word symposium has undergone, from the Greek word, meaning drinking and making merry together, to the English word, meaning a series of lectures or papers on the same subject.

Men in ancient Greece had quite different amusements from those of later times and places. But it is astonishing how similar the games and toys of Greek children of that day were to those of children of later ages. They built castles in the sand at the beach, rolled hoops, skipped rope, dressed and tended dolls made of wood with jointed arms and legs, played a game like jacks, flew kites, and played games similar to hopscotch, blindman's buff, and hide-and-seek. They had ball games and, for indoors, a game like checkers played on a squared-off board.

Little girls in Greece had games that involved dancing to songs like our nursery rhymes. One of these seems to have been somewhat like ring-around-a-rosy. One girl, or group of girls, asks:

> *Where are my roses?*
> *Where are my violets?*
> *Where is my beautiful parsley?*

and other children answer:

> *Here are your roses.*
> *Here are your violets.*
> *Here is your beautiful parsley.*

Another children's song shows that even our Halloween custom of "trick or treat" is thousands of years old. Children on the Greek island of Rhodes dressed as swallows on New Year's Day, and appeared at the doors of neighbors singing these three verses:

> *Roll us out a plum cake,*
> *For the swallows' sake . . .*
> *And wine in a flasket*
> *And cheese in a basket . . . .*

Boy rolling his hoop. This was a popular children's game in 500 B.C. The drawing is taken from a painted cup of that time

A young flute player with his dog. From the painting on a wine jar, 470 B.C.

If you shall say us nay
Then we will carry your door away,
Or the lintel above it, or easiest of all
Your wife herself, for she is but small.

But if something you bring
May it be a fine thing. . . .
Open the door to the swallows, then,
For we are children and not old men.

Ω *ω* is for **Ωκεανος**, or in English letters *Okeanos* (pronounced *oh-kay-ah-nóss*), the god Okeanos.

Okeanos was one of the very ancient Greek gods, the lord of the ocean and the son of Ouranos, the heavens, and of Ge, the earth. From him were descended all streams, rivers, fountains, and brooks. He is pictured as a gentle, hospitable old man, but was a hazy personality about whom there were few myths. He early faded into obscurity, superseded by Poseidon, the powerful god of the sea.

Okeanos was almost forgotten as a god, but remained always important to the Greeks as an idea. They believed that a great river called Okeanos flowed completely around the earth. This outer region, beyond the known and civilized world, was an alarming place filled with monstrous creatures, like gorgons and dragons. The entrance to the underworld of Hades was on the shores of Okeanos, and all the people who lived in lands adjoining his waters were weird and strange. As the Greeks acquired more knowledge of geography, Okeanos became more and more the great salt ocean to the west, beyond the Mediterranean. But this western ocean was still an uncharted, mysterious, and frightening place, where even Heracles dared not go.

Herodotus was the only Greek writer who traveled widely and described the countries of the ancient world. He related tall tales (perhaps with tongue in cheek), but he was a keen observer and could sift out the truth buried in sailors' and explorers' yarns, which were all that was known of much of the earth. He dismissed the idea that Okeanos encircled the world, saying, "I know of no river called Ocean." As to whether the ocean extended along the west and to the north of Europe, he said that he had never been able to get a report from anyone who had seen it. He described the known world, which the Greeks called the *oikoumene* (a word related to *oikos*, "house") as consisting of Europe, Asia, and Africa. He said that in Europe the Danube River made its northern boundary, and that he was told that no one could live farther north than the Danube because of great numbers of bees that swarmed there. Herodotus scoffed at this. He said that bees could not

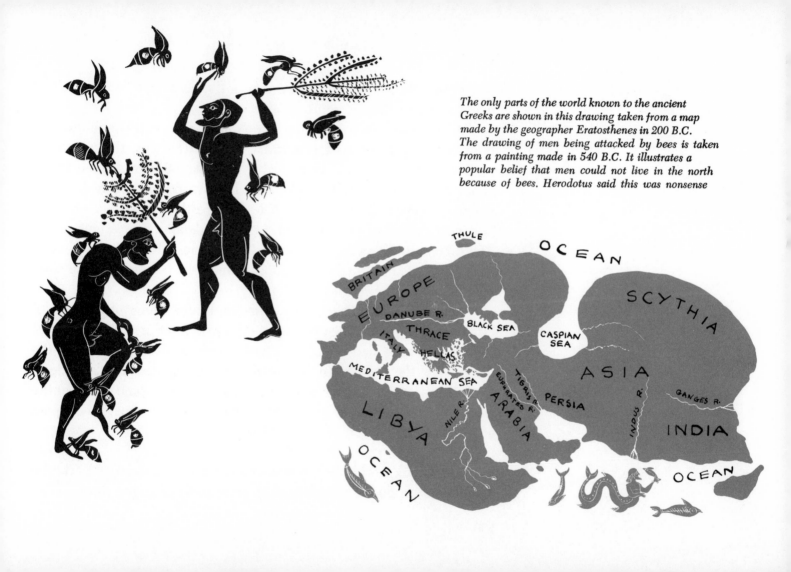

The only parts of the world known to the ancient Greeks are shown in this drawing taken from a map made by the geographer Eratosthenes in 200 B.C. The drawing of men being attacked by bees is taken from a painting made in 540 B.C. It illustrates a popular belief that men could not live in the north because of bees. Herodotus said this was nonsense

OCEAN

THULE

BRITAIN

EUROPE

DANUBE R.

THRACE

ITALY

HELLAS

BLACK SEA

SCYTHIA

CASPIAN SEA

ASIA

MEDITERRANEAN SEA

EUPHRATES R.

TIGRIS R.

PERSIA

INDUS R.

GANGES R.

LIBYA

NILE R.

ARABIA

INDIA

OCEAN

OCEAN

live in so cold a climate, so that it was the cold itself, not bees, that made northern Europe uninhabitable.

Asia and Africa were better known to the Greeks. Herodotus said that Asia was settled as far as India, but "farther east the country is uninhabited and nobody knows what it is like." He had much to say about Africa, which the Greeks called Libya. He had traveled over much of Egypt and wrote of the Nile and of Ethiopia with much accurate information as well as some fantastic details. The extent of the African continent was not known in Greek times, although the Phoenicians had sailed far down both the east and west coasts and even completely around the southern end.

Most Greeks of Herodotus's time, and later, clung to the idea of Okeanos as a great river marking the outside limit of everything. But they would have had no quarrel with Herodotus's boundaries of the *oikoumene:* the Danube to the north, India to the east, the latitude of the headwaters of the Nile to the south, and the fearsome ocean to the west. Of that inhabited world, they themselves, of course, occupied only a portion.

The Greek world, then, was a small one. But inside that world the inhabitants produced a society that profoundly changed all societies that followed. They peopled their small world with nymphs and gods and goddesses like none that were ever conceived before. They left behind many other wonderful things.

At the height of their greatness they produced the Parthenon and its fine sculptures, and the vitality of that temple symbolized the rich contribution of the city of Athens. She gave us the idea of government by private citizens, united by a passionate involvement in the politics of their city, and the idea of theater presenting dramas of intense emotion for the whole population to experience together. Athens was also the city where, for awhile, men walked the streets, confident that by debate they could find the truth and solve all the puzzles of the universe.

The Athens of the wonderful theater and the great philosophers lasted only a brief time. Much of our Greek heritage comes from many small, scattered Hellenic cities. For centuries before the rise of Athens to a dominating position, these cities produced lovely poetry and works of art, and new ideas that broke the barriers of ancient superstitions. For it was the Greeks who turned the world toward reasonable explanation of the problems of medicine, mathematics, and other sciences. They had a society that left them free to use their minds and encouraged them to do so.

Eos, goddess of the dawn, sprinkling the earth with dew. From a painted oil jar

This freedom of thought—this adventurousness of the mind—is the primary quality that made possible the Greek contributions to later ages. If we could somehow go back and live among the ancient Greeks, we should be aware of other qualities, less pleasing than those that underlie their great achievements. The Greeks had their full share of faults and disagreeable traits, and perhaps more than their share of some. They were known for wily tricks and cunning stratagems and for self-seeking—a self-seeking that sometimes led to seizing a neighbor or his goods in a quick raid. But fortunately for the world, they had more than their share, too, of the superior qualities that are evident in their creations.

The Greeks lived in a youthful time of the world's history, and in a land of intense and brilliant sunshine. When we look at the things they made we can sense something of the sunlit mornings of that early world, and of the people, adventurous and unafraid, who created lasting gifts for mankind.

Athenian youth on his prancing horse.
The inscription says: "Leandros is
handsome." Drawing from a painted cup
of 500 B.C.

Acknowledgments

The author and publisher wish to thank the following companies for permission to quote selections from their publications:

"Headdress," by Sappho, from *Greek Lyric Poetry*, translated by Willis Barnstone. Copyright © 1962, 1967 by Bantam Books, Inc. This appears on page 67; from Homer, *The Odyssey*, translated by Robert Fitzgerald. Copyright © 1961 by Robert Fitzgerald. Reprinted by permission of Doubleday & Company, Inc. Two excerpts, pages 49 and 51; from *The Splendor of Greece*, by Robert Payne. Copyright © 1960 by Harper & Row, Publishers, Inc. This appears on page 90; from *Great Dialogues of Plato*, translated by W. H. D. Rouse and edited by Philip G. Rouse and Eric R. Warmington. Copyright © 1956, 1961 by John Clive Graves Rouse. Reprinted by arrangement with The New American Library, Inc., New York. These appear on pages 35 and 92; from *Approach to Greek Art*, by Charles Seltman. Copyright © 1960 by The Viking Press, Inc., Publishers. These appear on pages 78 and 120. The other Greek translations that appear in the book were done by the author.

Grateful acknowledgment is also given to the following sources for the use of the photographs and for the use of the museum pieces from which Winifred Lubell made the drawings.

The photographs are from: Acropolis Museum, Athens, 85; Bolton, Lee, 120; British Museum, London, 88, 113; Greece News Bureau, New York, 86; The Metropolitan Museum of Art, New York, 73 (Rogers Fund, 1947), 74 (artists, Rogers Fund, 1950), 75 (Fletcher Fund, 1932), 76 (wreath, Gift of J. Pierpont Morgan, 1900), 81 (making cakes, Fletcher Fund, 1931), 83 (Fletcher Fund, 1931), 104 (Purchase, 1942, Joseph Pulitzer Bequest); Museum of Fine Arts, Boston, 56 (Gift of Mrs. W. Scott Fitz), 74 (statue, Pierce Fund), 76 (earring), 81 (grating cheese, woman and child), 104; National Museum, Athens, 51; Staatliche Antikensammlungen und Glyptothek, Munich, 47; Staatliche Museen, Berlin, 76 (statue); Wadsworth Atheneum, Hartford, Connecticut, 95.

The drawings are from: American School of Classical Studies, Athens, 123 (boy and dog); Ashmolean Museum, Oxford, England, 29 (sandalmaker), 125; British Museum, London, 15 (wrestlers, javelin thrower), 17, 21, 23, 49, 91, 94, 99, 101, 108 (comedy mask), 115, 123 (cockfight), 129; Cabinet des Médailles, Paris, 7; Collection of E. G. Spencer-Churchill, 60; Herakleion Museum, Crete, 59; Lindenau Museum, Altenburg, Germany, 123 (boar hunt); The Louvre, Paris, 2, 29 (wine cart), 35, 39, 43, 45, 66, 69 (man and trees, rabbits), 97, 131; The Metropolitan Museum of Art, New York, 10 (Rogers Fund, 1914), 18, 55 (Helios, Bellerophon and Pegasus), 63, 82 (Fletcher Fund, 1931), 102 (nursing bottle, wine cup), 111; Museo Archeologico, Florence, 55 (centaur), 93; Museo Archeologico Nationale, Ferrara, 109; Museo Archeologico Nationale, Naples, 105; Museo Arqueologico Nacional, Madrid, 79; Museo Mandralisca, Cefalu, Sicily, 29 (fish store); Museum of Fine Arts, Boston, 13, 15 (charioteer, discus thrower), 19, 64, 65, 71, 72, 118; National Museum, Athens, 31, 33, 41, 52, 108 (tragedy mask), 117; Palermo Museum, Sicily, 126; Petit Palais, Paris, 69 (sheep and goat), 116; Royal Museum, Brussels, 80; Schwerin Museum, Germany, 61; Staatliche Antikensammlungen, Munich, 133; Staatliche Museen, Berlin, 15 (racers), 25, 67, 102 (perfume flask), 107; Tarquinia National Museum, Italy, 40, 121; Torno Collection, Milan, 102 (potter); Vlastos Collection, Athens, 26.

The maps on pages 37 and 129 were drawn by Winifred Lubell.

For Further Reading

Alsop, Joseph W. *From the Silent Earth*. New York: Harper & Row, 1964.

Asimov, Isaac. *The Greeks: A Great Adventure*. Boston: Houghton Mifflin, 1965.

———. *Words from the Myths*. Boston: Houghton Mifflin, 1961.

Auden, W. H., ed. *The Portable Greek Reader*. New York: Viking Press, 1948.

Boardman, John. *Greek Art*. New York: Praeger, 1964.

Bowra, Cecil M. *The Greek Experience*. New York: Mentor Books, 1957.

Downey, Glanville, ed. *Stories From Herodotus*. New York: Dutton, 1965.

Finley, M. I. *The Ancient Greeks*. New York: Viking Press, 1963.

Fitts, Dudley, ed. *Greek Plays in Modern Translation*. New York: Dial, 1947.

Fitzgerald, Robert. *The Odyssey of Homer*. New York: Doubleday, 1961.

Glubok, Shirley. *The Art of Ancient Greece*. New York: Atheneum, 1963.

Graves, Robert. *The Greek Myths*, 2 vols. Baltimore: Penguin Books, 1955.

Grene, David, and Lattimore, Richmond, eds. *Greek Tragedies,* 3 vols. Chicago: University of Chicago Press, 1960.

Hale, William H. *The Horizon Book of Ancient Greece*. New York: Doubleday, 1965.

Hall, Jennie. *Buried Cities*. New York: Macmillan, 1964.

Hamilton, Edith. *The Greek Way*. New York: Modern Library, 1930.

———. *Mythology*. New York: Mentor Books, 1940.

Hooper, Finley. *Greek Realities*. New York: Scribners, 1966.

Kitto, H. D. F. *The Greeks*. Baltimore: Penguin Books, 1951.

Larousse Encyclopedia of Mythology. New York: Putnam, 1959.

Lattimore, Richmond. *The Iliad of Homer*. Chicago: University of Chicago Press, 1951.

Lloyd-Jones, Hugh, ed. *The Greek World*. Baltimore: Penguin Books, 1962.

MacKendrick, Paul. *The Greek Stones Speak*. New York: St. Martin's Press, 1962.

Oates, Whitney J., and Murphy, Charles T., eds. *Greek Literature in Translation*. New York: David McKay, 1944.

Price, Christine. *Made in Ancient Greece*. New York: Dutton, 1967.

Quennell, Marjorie and Charles H. *Everyday Things in Ancient Greece*. New York: Putnam, 1967.

Richter, Gisela. *A Handbook of Greek Art*. London: Phaidon, 1959.

Seltman, Charles. *Approach to Greek Art*. New York: Dutton, 1960.

Index

138

143